Diary Of A Common Man

Dr. Raj

Foreword by Dr C. Jayakumar, CHRO, L&T

ISBN 979-8-89610-658-6

Cover Design: Jaya Niyathi
Graphic Design: Madhan

Author's E-mail: drrajwrites@gmail.com

---◆◇◆---

*I want to thank my parents, teachers,
family, friends...and so on...*

*Frankly I do not know who and what to
exclude in expressing my gratitude*

*I thank life for everything it has given me...
without life and its depth, there is no diary!*

---◆◇◆---

Contents

Contents

Foreword

In a career spanning nearly four decades in the field of HR, I've had the privilege of engaging with many who share a passion for leadership and personal growth, each with their own unique story. Yet, few have left as indelible a mark as Dr. Raj, the author of the book you now hold.

My association with Dr. Raj began almost a decade ago. From our first interaction, I was drawn to his knowledgeable yet humble demeanour. Raj's innate ability to connect with people, coupled with his genuine and nuanced communication style, left a lasting impression on me. He struck me as someone who doesn't just speak about values - he lives them. Dr. Raj's sincerity and warmth shine through in everything he does. These traits make him well-suited to pen a book like *Diary of a Common Man*.

In a series of fifty insightful episodes that shaped Dr. Raj's perspective on life, he candidly reflects on moments many might overlook as ordinary, yet brings out their deeper meanings with extraordinary clarity. Dr. Raj's writing is simple and relatable, inviting the reader to walk alongside him through various phases of life. It's a testament to how common lives reveal uncommon wisdom when viewed through a thoughtful lens.

In reading this book, you'll find numerous stories that resonate with the struggles, joys, and challenges of everyday people. When I read *Diary of a Common Man*, I was struck by the authenticity and warmth that permeate every page. There is no pretence, no exaggeration—just a heartfelt account of a journey that is at once unique and universal. It is this sincerity that makes the book a compelling read and a valuable resource for self-reflection.

In one of the chapters, he narrates his experiences during his university days - a period marked not by privilege but by perseverance. Living in modest accommodation, navigating less-than-ideal conditions and finding support in the most unexpected places, Raj and his friends formed an unbreakable bond. These stories are a vivid reminder that a positive environment and the right mindset can transform challenges into triumphs.

Dr. Raj's life has been devoted to uplifting everyone he encounters, with a natural talent for coaching and nurturing that consistently exceeds expectations. His diary serves not only as a record of his own experiences but as a guiding light, inspiring readers to reflect upon their own journeys. His focus on self-awareness and introspection encourages readers to pause and reflect on their own lives, finding significance in everyday experiences. Through practical wisdom and live examples, he imparts lessons that resonate deeply, leaving a lasting impact on all who read them.

When Dr. Raj approached me to write the foreword for his book, I was genuinely honoured. My initial hesitation was quickly swept away by his conviction and enthusiasm - a reflection of the passion that he has poured into this work. It is a privilege to introduce *Diary of a Common Man* to you, dear readers, and I am confident that you will find as much value in it as I did. Thank you, Raj, for allowing me this honour and for sharing your story with the world.

I would like to reiterate that this book is a journey - one that invites its readers to pause, reflect, and explore their own lives through a renewed perspective. To sum up, I am reminded of this beautiful quote:

> *"The simple things are also the most extraordinary things, and only the wise can see them."*
>
> –Paulo Coelho

Happy reading and reflecting!

Dr. C. Jayakumar
Executive Vice President & CHRO
Larsen & Toubro Limited

Basic Premise

I am a common man. There are many like me around. You may then wonder why I should write a diary and why anyone should be interested in reading it. Let me present my logic.

Since I am a common man, I was taking an ordinary look at my life. I also discovered that *not taking* an introspective look at myself and my life is also quite common. Occasionally, I paused and pondered. The moment I started looking deeper at my life and experiences, I kept finding some valuable insights that helped me better understand myself and my life. I documented my experiences and insights for further reflection. That is how **Diary of a Common Man** was born!

Since there are many common people like me, I thought that my diary might interest them and that they could relate to it. My desire here is to see many more common people like me take an uncommon look at their lives. *We will most likely discover extraordinary things from our ordinary lives.*

How to Read This Book?

Simple. Just pick up any chapter and enjoy the anecdote or experience.

I have not kept any chronological dependencies so you can choose any chapter in any order. Also, I have kept these chapters quite crisp so that you can complete reading them in 5 to 6 minutes and spend another 5 to 6 minutes contemplating the content you read. About 10 to 12 minutes will be enough to read one chapter. By then, you must be slipping into your sleep.

My intention is to keep this reading very light yet stimulate personal introspection. Reflection, introspection, contemplation, etc., should not scare us away. We need to keep them simple.

All the chapters are real and straight from my life. In a few places, I took the real or disguised names of a few people in my life, and in most other places, I did not mention names because my focus was more on ME than on them.

Enjoy the light read and deep thought!

1

Die Empty

My mind has never been idle; it keeps reflecting and generating thoughts, ideas, desires, wish lists, etc. I have been very fond of small pocketbooks, electronic diaries, and mobile apps such as Mind Notes, One Note, Google Keep, etc. I used them to record all the ideas that I wanted to explore, all the articles, blogs, or books that I wanted to write, and all the self-care that I wanted to initiate.

So far, so good. The disturbing question that keeps popping up is: How many of them have I worked on, progressed on, or completed? Needless to say, it is a very small percentage. My mind generates more things to do than what my self-discipline enables me to execute. Soon, I realized that personal accountability is indeed a rare quality that I need to nurture, without which I would be disappointing myself.

I specifically say personal accountability because I realized that I was very consciously accountable to my bosses, clients, and teams. Thankfully, my accountability towards others was intact and always pushed me to fulfil my commitments. But when it comes to working on things that others do not chase me, I lack personal accountability.

In my defence, I can attribute my lack of personal accountability to all the distractions around me, other priorities or lack of time. Honestly, these are mere excuses. The deeper reason could be a lack of instant consequence or gratification.

When I commit something to my boss, client or team, they will follow up with me if I do not meet my commitments. If I do a good job for them, they might acknowledge or there is a sense of accomplishment. It is gratifying. On the contrary, who will nudge me if I do not work on things I commit to myself?

For example, if I do not do physical exercise, who will push me? If I do not write this book, who will ask me? If I do not read the latest writings in my field, who cares? If I do not clean my desk or wardrobe, who is bothered? These situations call for personal accountability because there is no external nudge or gratification—at least not instantly!

I realized that to work on things with personal accountability, one would require a high level of self-awareness and discipline.

Self-awareness involves developing a sense of purpose; it should answer the question to myself: why do I want to commit to doing things that others may not nudge me about? If I develop a clear sense of purpose, my internal engine will be activated, improving my personal accountability.

Another factor that can enhance my personal accountability is a set of routines and sticking to them. For example, I can postpone my writing indefinitely because no publisher is behind me. Or I can keep a routine to write 500 words every morning with my coffee before I get into the rest of the daily responsibilities. If I pursued this routine for 100 days, for example, I would have ended up writing at least 50,000 words. It is all about habit formation!

While there could be many more tricks, I shortlisted a deep sense of purpose and a simple routine as the workable tricks to induce personal accountability within me. In addition, it will also help to develop a network of people around me who are pursuing things with passion. Such an environment will be pretty stimulating and will act as a nudge. Of course, it is still a work in progress for me.

Finally, if I do not want to look back at my life with regret over a long list of unattended things to do, I need to pump up my personal accountability!

I am reminded of this beautiful book - Die Empty - by Todd Henry!

2

Allow Books to Speak

Back then, my pastime on a Sunday morning was driving my two-wheeler to a road near the Head Post office and roaming around for a few hours. My main attraction was the heap of books on the pavement that were on second sale.

My eyes kept scanning the wide scatter of books. I was not looking for anything specific except to find something interesting. One title caught my attention. I picked it up and found it was available for a throwaway price of 100 rupees. I quietly paid and bought the book. I was eager to read the book, so I curtailed my further search and went home.

Over the years, I realized how that one book had a profound impact on the choices that I made in my life. Thanks to Charles Handy for inspiring me through that book – The Hungry Spirit!

In particular, a chapter called the "Doctrine of Enough" made me think and evaluate what I wanted to do with my life. The essence of that chapter is that unless you

I felt uncomfortable with myself. How can a teacher, who is supposed to be a well-wisher, develop such an envious attitude towards a student?

Did that feeling of jealousy prompt me to take risks and grow in my career? Subconsciously, yes! It's not just this episode; I can recall several such instances. I never liked to be compared with others. If I was compared and if I felt smaller, it created that 'extra' drive in me to get better.

Reflecting now, I realize that even a negative emotion, when appropriately channelled, yields positive results!

What negative emotions am I carrying at present? How can I regulate them to give me positive energy?

10

Discern During Desperation

It was those days that I will remember forever! Too much was happening in my life at that time.

I was into full-time teaching in Mumbai. I was enjoying the challenge and students were receiving my lectures well. The going was good until I was diagnosed with symptoms that were close to tuberculosis (which had a lot of stigma, more than the medical problem). I was experiencing sudden bouts of high fever, and I was losing weight big time. Diagnosis also got delayed until another senior professor took me to his family physician, who accidentally touched my neck and felt the swollen lymph nodes. I did not know how to react when the doctor said that it could lead to TB!

On the career front, I was making attempts to move from teaching into the corporate sector. I applied for a few opportunities, and one of them clicked pretty soon. I was impressed with the way I cracked the interview in corporate sectors—more so after I was branded as a 'faculty' who might not fit into the corporate world!

The icing on the cake was getting the corporate position back in my hometown. It would be a reunion with my parents!

Honestly, my parents did not bother to ask what the salary was. They were happy that I was coming home; they wanted me to pay attention to my health. They were so concerned that they asked me to quit the Mumbai job and take a break.

I requested a month to join the new job. I had this time to recoup and regain my confidence. It was a good time to get pampered!

Then came a call from my new company, asking me about a date for my pre-employment medical examination! I experienced a chilling fear through my spine.

What if the medical examination revealed my lymph node infection? Will it be a reason to disqualify me? Will I be left jobless? What will be my future? Should I tell the doctor about my problem and ask for suggestions? Will he understand my concern, or will he report back to the company? I must confess that during my desperate moments, I entertained the thought of bribing the doctor to write a favourable report. But I could not muster the courage to do so! Fortunately, I was meek!

Will I at least get to see the report? I was told no. It goes directly to the company. Will the company inform me immediately about my disqualification, or will they wait until my joining day?

The one-month break before joining the new job meant for my rest turned out to be a very restless time indeed!

Most reluctantly, I went to the designated hospital.

The nursing staff, path lab technicians, and doctors went through the process as a routine. They see hundreds of people every day. For me, however, it was a life-defining medical examination!

It was over. Deep in my heart, I felt it was all over. That was the end of my dream of getting into the corporate sector. Should I head back to Mumbai and rejoin my teaching?

There were a few days left for me to join the new company if they did not disqualify me based on my medical report.

Every day, I waited with utter disgust for bad news to come my way. It did not.

Should I report to my new job? How should I take it if they reject me then?

On D-day, I got ready. Instead of happiness, I was filled with fear—fear of rejection!

I pushed myself to the new office. An executive welcomed me and gave me a simple form to fill in.

It was my joining report.

Hurray, I was not rejected! I am not jobless. I entered the corporate sector!

My new life had just begun!

Looking back, I realize that the fear multiplied in my mind than in reality. I also learned that in those testing moments, healthy and unhealthy options cross our minds. It was critical not to lose the ability to distinguish between a good practice and a bad practice. Desperation drives one to opt for apparently easy choices. But they could create a lasting negative impact. One temptation of bribing the doctor would have ruined my career, who knows! Deep down there is an ethical compass within each one of us; so long as we keep it activated, we will be able to discern right or wrong and act accordingly.

11

First Flight & Early Learning

My first flight was such a big issue!

By Indian standards, I was told that I grew faster to become the head of the Management Department in a world-bank-funded research organization.

Two things attracted me to take up this opportunity. The big factor was the World Bank's funding support to build the organization and carry out field research in public systems. The second factor was heading the department at a young age! I don't know why, but there is always an eagerness to take up bigger responsibility. Does it symbolize faster growth?

Frankly, I was learning on the job and did not even know of my authority or eligibility for various entitlements. I was so excited about my research trips to the interior areas. For someone who had previously spent time within the four walls of a classroom teaching MBA students, field research was certainly a new learning experience.

On one occasion, a top-level official from the ministry suggested that I visit another Institute of national reputation based in Mumbai. Not knowing my eligibility, I started enquiring about various trains. The administrative officer asked why I was not opting for a flight instead of a train! On enquiry, he told me that under some government rules, people working on World Bank-sponsored projects are treated at par with some senior-grade officers in the Government. I wanted to reconfirm my flight eligibility, but there was little time as I had to travel at short notice.

The Administrative Officer was pretty persuasive. He encouraged me to go ahead with my flight tickets and suggested that I claim reimbursement on my return.

Let me admit—the thought of flying for the first time was also exciting. I booked my air tickets.

The subsequent tension was familiarising myself with airport procedures and in-flight manners. Being a first-time flyer, I was very self-conscious. Luckily for me, my neighbour was also flying on the same day and on the same flight. She was a senior lady and well experienced in flying across the globe. She gave me so much comfort and helped during my first flight. From the check-in process and security check to fastening seat belts, she guided me. Thanks to her help, I carried myself like a pro!

After successful meetings in Mumbai, I flew back only to find myself in big soup.

The deputy director (nominated by the government to the World Bank-sponsored research institute), who was the administrative officer's boss, raised concerns about my flying. I submitted my reimbursement claim only to be chided by him for not consulting him before booking.

Being prompted by the administrative officer, I referred to some rule that allows people in my grade to fly. He was even more upset. He asked me to go and get a copy of the GO (Government Order) with the mention of such a rule. Until then, he said that the file would not move.

I was stuck very badly. The to-and-fro airfare was equal to half of my monthly salary. I spent from my pocket and was struggling to get back. The administrative officer, with a nice diplomatic smile, excused himself and instead asked me to deal with his boss directly.

After a few occasions of waiting outside his room and many discussions with the Deputy Director, his ego was restored while I shed some of mine. At last, he signed the reimbursement file with a stern warning that I should not make decisions without consulting him.

I had a sigh of relief at getting my money back.

My first flight experience also gave me my first encounter with bureaucracy! Rules alone cannot save you unless you learn to balance relationships. Managing own ego as well as others is a necessary art.

12

Respect What We Have

Ours was a middle-class family, requiring both my parents to work to make a living. Interestingly, during my early college days or growing up, I never knew that we were having financial challenges. I must give full credit to my parents, who never allowed those monetary constraints to surface to impact my sister or me. Within those means, my parents always gave us those experiences that were memorable.

In our simple living during those days, our way of celebrating any achievement was to go out to eat and watch a movie. One such occasion was when I cleared my Intermediate course (equivalent to 12th class) with first-class marks – that too in English medium! Surprisingly, after checking my results and seeing that I cleared the course, I instantly turned sober. A sense of calm or silence dawned inside me. There was no vivid expression on my face, no jubilation, no brisk body language, nor any joyful celebration. After tasting success, I still cannot figure out that reaction in my demeanor. I'm not sure if success humbled me or if that was my way of relieving the stress and feeling light!

Despite my restrained reaction to my success, my Dad insisted on taking me out to a movie to celebrate. That was his way of appreciating my achievement and expressing his happiness; otherwise, he is also a man of few expressions and more actions.

We all went to a theatre and stood in the queue to buy tickets. Yes, in those days, we had no online ticket booking using mobile wallets. We had to experience the anxiety of standing in the queue and hoping that tickets wouldn't be sold out by the time we neared the ticket counter. That anxiety was a part of the entire movie-going experience!

My Dad and I were standing in the queue for a 'First Class' ticket – a category of ticket that gets a seat towards the rear of the auditorium, with a good view. While we were waiting for the counter to open, I had an unexpected friend waving at me from a distance. Sunil was standing in another queue, a little away from where we were.

That queue belonged to the 'Balcony' class – the highest priced ticket that possibly offered a 'royal view'. I waved back briefly and turned my head away from Sunil. For a fraction of a second, I imagined Sunil judging me and my family for not going for the balcony's royal view. Not to entertain this thought any further, I focused on my 'first class' ticket counter.

I didn't notice what my Dad was doing. But he did catch my faint feelings and mild discomfort. Perhaps he did not want me to feel any less than my friends regarding status. Going for a balcony viewing was considered to be 'high class,' and so Dad offered to change the queue. He suggested that all of us would go for a balcony royal view by paying a higher price. Obviously, he intended to make me feel on par with my friend Sunil and no less.

My instant response to my Dad's suggestion of changing the queue is still fresh in my mind. I replied with a blunt NO and insisted on going for 'first class' view only. Honestly, I could not analyze deeply why I reacted that way, but my stand liberated me from my discomfort, and I started looking at Sunil with a smile and waved again.

This episode stayed with me for so long because perhaps I had learnt some interesting insights (honestly, I didn't realize during those days). Accepting what you are and what you have and feeling good about it is essential. While we must strive to improve and grow, it is also important to value what we have and be content with that—more so when such symbols of status are so superficial and transient.

A person who has no money to use any transport uses foot to commute; another earns to use public transport; some others own a bicycle, someone else a bike or car and so on. While striving to move from one to the other is a sign of growth, feeling terrible with what you have leads to misery. It is like a person flying by economy class feeling ashamed after seeing another friend flying business class! I wonder why – at that moment, we don't think of the person who commutes on foot!

13

Once Cheated, Never Trust

Secunderabad railway station, evening 6 pm.

It was a busy station and we, as a family, were about to board the train to Tirupati, a pilgrimage destination. After settling down with my family at the respective reserved places in the coach, I got down to buy a bottle of water.

I bought the water and turned back to go to the coach. It was then that I saw this gentleman standing near me and just greeted me, saying 'hello'. I wondered if I knew this person or if I had met this person before. I looked at him more closely, trying to recollect.

He was fair–looking, with curly—but ruffled—hair and spectacles. He was wearing dark-colored trousers with a plain-colored shirt tucked in. Overall, he came across as a person in executive attire but with a tired look. When you look at him closely, you can see a few marks of dirt on his shirt—he might have been traveling from a long distance.

As he greeted me, I paused and looked at him. He took a couple of steps towards me, and it was then that I noticed a slight limp in his walk. He introduced himself as Murthy, a native of Tirupati town. As a courtesy, I introduced myself too and told him about my pilgrimage trip to Tirupati with family. He wished me a good trip and offered his help in case I needed any support in Tirupati. Our conversation was all in English—just like in a corporate environment.

My wife and Dad were watching me from the train – perhaps wondering why I was taking so long to buy a water bottle.

As I was about to excuse myself, Murthy asked me to stay for another minute and said he had something important to talk about. I wondered what we had in common, but I stayed there.

He then asked me if I heard of the train accident during the early hours of that day. I said yes, and it was a train going to Shirdi, another pilgrimage destination. Then he revealed that he was one of the many on that ill-fated train and had a miraculous escape by God's grace. He slightly lifted his trousers to show me the heavily banded calf muscle due to injury. I could see bloodstains on the white bandage, and I felt sad for how much pain he might be undergoing. I also could understand the reason for the limp in his walk.

He said, he somehow returned to Secunderabad, and now he was waiting for the next special train to travel to his hometown, Tirupati. He also shared how he lost his luggage and all his belongings and barely escaped from death. I remember hearing about a few people losing lives in that morning accident. He folded his hands and said, "Somehow, by God's blessings, I am still alive to return to my family".

I wished him a safe journey and was about to walk towards the train, as it was time for my train's departure. Murthy hurriedly limped towards me and quickly asked if I could lend him some money to buy a ticket to Tirupati and that he would meet me in Tirupati at my hotel and return the money.

For a moment, I hesitated. He then searched his pocket and, pulled out his business card and showed me his phone number in Tirupati. He said, "I will be reaching Tirupati by the next train, and it will be 4 hours later than yours. If you could call me on this phone number tomorrow evening, I will come to your hotel and return the money. This is just a professional help. I feel awkward to ask you like this, but I am helpless after losing all my belongings and barely escaping death".

My wife was curiously looking through the train window wondering who was speaking with me. Murthy was standing in front of me – certainly looking uncomfortable asking for money from a stranger.

There was an announcement that my train was about to depart.

Murthy said, "if you cannot trust me in this situation, then leave it. I will wait for someone to help me. I am so desperate, and I have stooped to this level of almost begging. I don't know why Shirdi Baba punished me like this". His English was fluent, yet emotional.

I quickly took out my wallet and shared two 500-rupee notes. I told him I would call him the next evening and ran to the train as it was about to depart. I didn't even look back at Murthy because I didn't want to see his expression of embarrassment.

As I sat in my seat, my Dad asked me what had happened. I told him briefly about Murthy and how I gave him some money, which he would return the next day. When I said this, my Dad's reaction surprised me. I thought my Dad would be happy to see me helping someone in dire need. Instead, he turned skeptical and said, "This kind of people could be cheating. You should not have given money".

Somehow, I didn't like his reaction, so I remained quiet. Later, I told my wife, "If we don't help another human being in such a desperate situation, are we human?" She could not take a stand between my Dad and me; she just smiled!

We arrived in Tirupati the next morning, and we spent the whole day visiting religious places in that temple town. Towards the evening, my wife reminded me that I should call Murthy.

While my parents were relaxing in the hotel room, my wife and I stepped out to make a call. They were the days before I owned a mobile phone. We were still using a public telephone to make and pay per call. I took out the business card that Murthy gave me and dialed the number. As I was dialing, I was mentally rehearsing the hotel address to share with him so that he could come down to return the money.

At first instance, I could not connect the number. I redialed, and after a few beeps, I heard the voice, "The number that you dialed doesn't exist. Please check the number and try again". Perhaps my expression changed; my wife worriedly asked, "What happened?". I didn't reply. Instead, I redialed – only to receive the same message. I rechecked the business card; it didn't have any other number or address. Some company name was printed, without any details.

So, was Murthy a cheat – as my Dad suspected?

I told my wife what had happened. We had to reconcile to the fact that we had been cheated. At that moment, I realized that the feeling of being cheated hurts more than losing money.

****

Almost one year passed since Murthy's episode. It was a Sunday, and I was in my bedroom with my Sunday newspaper when I heard my wife speaking to someone at the main door.

"If you can support me in any small way, I can pay my fee and appear for my exams. You know that my Dad cannot afford this expense, and I am very much interested in pursuing my studies. I thought you might be able to help."

I could recognize the voice. It was the son of a priest who performed the rituals at the temple near my house. My wife visited that temple frequently; thus, the priest's family was more acquainted with her. The priest was not doing well financially; their family used to live on meagre earnings. While his son went to a college, he occasionally helped his Dad perform temple rituals. I heard he was a bright student keen to pursue his education for a better future. Whenever my wife found him at the temple, she enquired about his studies and encouraged him to do well. For that reason, perhaps, he must have approached her.

When I heard that he requested financial support, my instinct was to ask how much he wanted. My wife started asking the same, and he mentioned some amount for the examination fee.

Even before my wife discussed or decided to offer support, my Dad overheard this conversation from the next room. He came out and said a blunt NO on our behalf. Dad also commented aloud that such requests for money may not be genuine and might not be used for the intended purpose. He also told him on his face how we were cheated a few months ago.

I remained stuck in my bedroom, unable to look at the young man's face. He must have been embarrassed and humiliated. He didn't say a single word and went away. My wife closed the door silently.

I was feeling terrible inside. This case might be genuine; we see them every day at the temple. The young man was struggling to pay for education, and a small help would lead to a better life. Why didn't we trust him and assist him?

We believe that our past experiences teach us and help us grow. But sometimes, our past could be baggage and would limit our future outlook by forming solid opinions.

One Murthy cheats me, and I stop trusting people. Do I allow one bad experience to change my character?

Should 'Once Cheated, Never Trust' be my slogan? Is this wisdom? Is this human? Should I not do things which I believe in and leave the rest to the character of others? Or should I judge people before and choose to help those who I think deserve it? How good am I at judging people? How right is it to mistrust people because I was cheated a few times? A lot to introspect....

14

Let Go – Feel Lighter

This episode took place in early 2001 when I was working in Bangalore, the darling location of the IT industry then, though I am not sure of it now.

Bangalore was and is a very happening city with buzzing Brigade Road and MG Road. However, my wife and I preferred other leisure activities than these busy roads. Our favorite leisure activity was shopping nearby or visiting a temple to enjoy the peaceful ambience.

We drove to a Hanuman (the monkey God) temple on one of the weekends. It was a Saturday, and I knew Hanuman temples would be crowded on Saturdays and Tuesdays. It was so crowded that I could not find a place to park. Leaving it on the roadside would be easy, but your mind gets preoccupied with the anxiety of police locking your car for parking on the road. The peaceful ambience of the temple would not help unless there is peace inside us!

I waited and got a place in the designated car park area. We also left our footwear at another counter with a proper token; otherwise, another anxiety of footwear theft. I never imagined that we would enter a temple carrying so many anxieties and pray for peace!

When I was placing the token inside my pocket, I noticed that my pocket was empty. My wallet was not there!

I suddenly experienced instant fear and it was chilling through my spine. Multiple thoughts crossed my mind all at once. Where did I lose it? Did someone flick it? How much money was in it? Did I keep the credit card also in my wallet?

My wife, who was walking a little ahead of me, turned back and looked at me and my hassled body language – fidgeting every part of my clothing to find the wallet. When she asked me, I said I lost my wallet, but I was not sure where. I replayed the series of events. I parked my car, walked towards the footwear counter and left behind my sandals. Did someone flick it in this short span?

My wife quickly remembered that I left it on the dining table at home. I quizzed her many times to reconfirm. Of course, I didn't know what else I could do if she was unsure. She gave a detailed narration of how we got ready, how we took out some coins of money for our use at the temple and then left behind the wallet while leaving the house. I could connect with that narration and was convinced that I left the wallet at home. I experienced sudden relief!

What I experienced during the rest of my stay at the temple premises was very interesting. My car and footwear were in a safe place. My pocket was empty without the wallet. I didn't have to tap my pocket often to check for the safety of my wallet. So, I didn't have anything to care and worry about. I suddenly felt light; I didn't have anything to hold onto; I could enjoy the moment; I could focus on my prayers; I didn't have any fear of losing anything. I paid closer attention to the rituals at the temple; I noticed the beauty of the flowers around the deity; I listened to the melodious payers.

Though I visited the temple several times, I never had experienced such an experience. That visit remained special.

When I didn't have anything to hold onto, I didn't fear losing anything. I felt lighter. I reflected and realized how it also applies to so many other occasions. Holding onto a position, power, greed, ego, negativity, bad relationship ... just leave them and the thoughts behind, without getting hooked onto them and without the fear of losing something. One can experience a new joy and peace that feels much lighter!

15

Hunger to Conquer or Greed

I had just gotten into my teens, perhaps studying in 6th or 7th grade. After school hours, we used to have some interesting local games – more earthy types of games and not the likes of cricket, shuttle badminton, basketball or video games. One such rustic game involved small to medium-sized glass balls - glass marbles - called 'golis' in Telugu.

The game with golis had many versions. A straightforward version involved two players; one throws a goli on the ground, some 3 to 4 meters distance. The second player then tries to hit that opponent's goli with his goli. If it hits the opponent's goli, then I own that opponent's goli and pocket it. If I miss hitting, then the opponent will get a chance to hit my goli from the position of his goli. Thus, we keep moving on the ground, covering some distance on the street as per our hits and misses. The ultimate goal is to win over as many golis as possible from the opponent.

My opponent was usually my neighboring friend, Purushothaman. Being a Tamilian, he attended an English-medium school while I attended a Telugu-medium school. Fortunately, he used to speak Telugu fluently and thereby became my friend. Besides many other sports, we were also into the goli game.

We usually stepped out of our houses wearing knickers and with a bunch of golis in our pockets, making a tingling noise.

On that evening, I stepped out to play with a bunch of new and old golis in my pocket – including my favourite goli – a glass goli with an orange leaf embedded in it. It was somewhat lighter than the other golis but nicely fitted in my hands, and it made it easy for me to hit the targeted goli of my opponent player consistently. In short, my orange goli was my lucky mascot!

After a quiet start to the game, my form picked up. I started hitting my opponent's golis regularly. And I felt my favorite orange goli also added to the magic – consistently hitting the target. Purushothaman was on the back foot and kept transferring the golis from his pocket to mine.

The joy of success was so intoxicating that it prompted me to go for it even more. I kept winning, and my pocket became heavier with the loads of golis I had won from

Purushothaman. I was the proud owner of two pocket loads now. I didn't know the business language then; had I known, I would have calculated the Return on Investment (ROI), which was a fabulous percentage.

Motivated by my form, I played longer than ever before. Late in the evening, it turned dark, and we could hardly see the golis. But we continued our game under a streetlight.

Purushothaman was looking jaded as he incurred heavy losses that day. He lost all his stock except one goli. I wanted to stop at that stage as we could hardly see the golis, and it was tough to hit the target like earlier.

Purushothaman was equally struggling with poor visibility, and he was tired due to heavy losses in the game. I could understand how it must have felt when he was down to one goli in his pocket! I felt a bit of empathy, though honestly, the feeling of victory was much stronger.

With a tired look on his face and dropped shoulders, Purushothaman proposed that we play for a few more minutes so that I could win the last goli from his hands and end the day on a great note. He also said, "The way you are playing today, this will be yours in a matter of minutes!", showing me his favorite big goli in glittering blue color!"

The way I played that day and the extent of my success until then were unimaginable. I was floating in that success. Given the mood, Purushothaman's proposal to play a few more minutes and win over the last goli sounded like a great idea. "Let the win be complete," my inflated ego prompted me!

We continued the game for a few more minutes. I failed to win over the last goli. Silently, Purushothaman won two golis back from me. He was having three and looked confident with renewed success.

At that moment, I proposed to stop the game as I could not see the goli and was not hitting it right. But Purushothaman refused to stop; he wanted to play faster as the tide turned in his favor.

Reluctantly, I continued, and he didn't stop for the next forty minutes. I lost all those I had won from Purushothaman, and we were back to what we started with.

We went back home with a wholly neutralized result. Honestly, I could not sleep that night. I kept reflecting on how I lost all that I won!

I didn't know this word then; otherwise, I would have surely described the entire episode as an example of greed! When I do not know where to draw contentment with success, greed overtakes. When I don't know how to manage my success, ego takes over, promptly leading me to failure!

16

Just Do It, They Will See It

Those days, I carried severe self-doubt (perhaps even today occasionally, though to a much lesser extent). When I think deeper, it may have been less about me and more about others, a belief that others knew more than me and that I was no match for them.

I vividly recall innumerable occasions when I remained quiet in several group settings —meetings, conferences, team outings, etc. Interestingly, I had something to say or contribute in all those situations but remained silent. Something held me back. Was it a fear of going wrong, fear of ridicule, or fear of humiliation? Now, if I look back, I don't think the fear was justified at all.

Fortunately, my fear was not so intense that I stayed away from such situations—though I didn't particularly welcome them either. When a larger purpose required me to be in a group setting, I attended - not participated! In hindsight, I believe that approach was a blessing in disguise. Otherwise, I would have completely shut myself off and avoided participation turning myself aloof.

Those who face similar fears may understand this better; it feels awful to be in a group setting, fighting internal battles to come out and express oneself. I went home regretfully on several occasions for not opening up and not contributing. The sense of regret created more gloom and made me even more sober for the next event. It was perpetuating!

Interestingly, the outward demeanour created an impression that I was a quiet hard worker and very honest in what I did. The image was that I was a reserved person who spoke less. Naturally, the external world had no problem with my self-doubt; it was only 'my' problem!

Years passed, and my self-doubt became an integral part of my personality. I knew I had to conquer this before it became too deep to uproot.

One specific event remained in my memory, which was a significant turning point in my fight with my self-doubt.

It was the Oberoi Towers in Mumbai. I registered for a 2-day training program by Dr TV Rao, the HR Guru. I reached the venue, and it was overwhelming. The aristocracy all around, graceful body language, and greetings of people around me made me shrink a bit more. I was very new to the five-star culture and global etiquettes (you appreciate more if you read about the surroundings in which my higher education took place). Internally, I was a fish out of water and externally, I was trying to put up a plastic smile (which people mistook as grace!).

Program started and I was into the topic, carefully listening to the discussions. As usual, I held the dialogue within myself and did not speak out. At one stage during the first session, I had a strong view on some topic and I wanted to share. I even articulated in my mind what I wanted to say. I scribbled on my notepad what was buzzing in my mind. But unknown fear held me back. I dabbled with my notes for a few minutes. My inner struggle intensified, and I experienced a strong urge to conquer my fear and express my views. I strongly felt that I had a perfect point to share.

In a few moments, my conviction about my thoughts became stronger than my fear of self-doubt. I did the unthinkable. I raised my hand to speak. Dr TV Rao encouraged me to share, and I did. Yes, I did speak and share, however stiff I was and however stiff my face might have been. To my own ears, my voice sounded very different than usual. But I spoke.

While the act of raising my hand and speaking up itself relieved me a lot and boosted my confidence, what happened during the next coffee break created utter disbelief!

People were surrounding Dr TV Rao and conversing with him inquisitively. I picked up a cup of coffee and moved to a corner quietly. Slightly away from the buzz, I was reminiscing what happened a while ago – I spoke and expressed. I was feeling happy with what I did. What helped me to open up? Was it my frustration with my self-doubt? Was it my confidence in my viewpoint? Was it my attempt to articulate in mind? Or, was it the scribble that I had on the note pad? I wanted to understand the success factor so that I could repeat my act.

As I was deep in my reflection, I saw someone nearing me with a big smile and greeting me. I exchanged pleasantries (I knew it was not that pleasant; it was a lot of effort). He was a handsome young man in a blazer with that extra fizz of confidence.

After a brief introduction, he said, "I was looking for you to tell you that I truly liked the point that you raised in the earlier session before the break. It made me think".

Excuse me... what did I hear? I spoke a few lines with tremendous effort, and this man appreciated it!

"I also wanted to check if you studied abroad", he continued. "I really enjoyed your diction and voice".

That was a little too much for me to take. I shared about my humble origins and schooling in Telugu medium, wanting to tone down his view of me.

After hearing about my background, he was even more shocked and impressed and praised me even more. I felt very shy and did not know how to receive those accolades. I knew that the young man was showering me with exaggerated compliments.

After a brief conversation, we returned to the session. I was sitting at the same place but with a different inner self. I could experience a rejuvenated feeling. That young man might have been liberal in appreciating; he might have been using his conversational skills to build rapport with people; it might have been a normal social conversation for him. But for me... it mattered a great deal! I needed that boost to believe in myself.

That young man would never realize what a difference he made to me, but I replayed and relived that conversation for a long time on several occasions to overcome my fears.

Unfortunately, in my anxiety, I didn't even register his name. He remained as 'that young man in a blazer' in my life pages!

Thank you, young man!

17

Hide Nothing, Feel No Guilt

If I were to compile a list of the most awkward situations I encountered, this would be among them. I still cannot understand why I did that, but I did.

It was those days when I was working for the Nagarjuna Group in Hyderabad. Having moved from academics, I quickly learned the corporate way of working and was doing well in my job. I enjoyed the job; I was zealous about coming up with new initiatives and delivering new training programs. I must say that my bosses and organization gave me tremendous freedom to perform my job.

When the going was good, I received an interesting enquiry. While the enquiry was exciting, my handling of it was totally wrong. I feel embarrassed and awkward just thinking about it now!

Shankar (his full name had another prefix to this, but for functional use, this is good enough) was a friend of my colleague – BS (full name again is irrelevant to the story). Shankar was freelancing for some training programs. One day, he brought a proposal to BS saying one of his clients wanted a training program, which he was uncomfortable delivering. He enquired if we would be interested in delivering. My colleague and I had the expertise and interest in the topic that Shankar mentioned. Shankar asked us to apply for leave from the office and deliver the program. In our excitement, we said yes!

We delivered one in Hyderabad and were happy with the feedback. Participants received the program very well. Then Shankar came back with the news that his client was delighted and wanted us to do this in Delhi for their other office also. BS and I hesitated because it would require us to be absent from work for two days, including travel; that too, both of us together would be conspicuous with our absence at the same time.

Shankar insisted that we deliver the program, saying he had to satisfy his client. We agreed reluctantly. BS and I decided to take different routes to apply for leave. BS would apply beforehand, and I would inform my boss that morning, claiming some emergency at home. This was the time the feeble reluctance started turning into discomfort within me!

Shankar organized our air tickets, and we reached Begumpet airport (it was then the Hyderabad airport— much smaller than what we have today). Our flight was to depart at 7.30pm or so. As I was waiting in the boarding area, an imaginary thought crossed my mind, and it grew monstrously in a few moments.

What if someone from my office sees us at the airport? What if they ask about our Delhi trip? What to tell them? What if they ask why BS and I are travelling together? How can I substantiate the fictitious *'emergency at home'* theory that I had to tell the next morning? Innumerable questions created a shiver in my spine. This uneasy thought haunted me until we boarded the flight without any known people noticing us.

It was about a two-hour flight, and after the first fifteen minutes, I was okay, just recovering from the earlier imagination. Before I could fully recover, another imaginary thought sprouted.

What if this flight met with an accident? What if we get injured? What if we are dead? Will they publish our names? Will they print out photographs? What if someone in Nagarjuna office sees those pictures? I know, now it sounds funny. But back then, it was killing me. I didn't know how to shut my mind.

As if the fear of thoughts was not enough, the flight went through severe turbulence for a while, making me again run through all the above questions.

During the flight, neither of us could discuss anything about the next day's program nor could I sleep. It was torturous.

At last, we landed safely and exited the Delhi airport without bumping into any known people.

It was almost half past ten in the night, and Delhi turned foggy, with poor visibility on the roads. We hired a cab (no Uber or Ola, just a normal old Fiat cab) and started to our destination. It was moving at a snail's pace, not so much due to traffic like today, but more due to thick fog making it difficult to drive on the road.

My imaginary thoughts recurred: What if this cab guy dashes into another vehicle? What if we have an accident in Delhi? What if it is a major accident or even fatal? I continued to imagine press coverage of our accident. Will the Hyderabad newspaper's edition carry news of accidents in Delhi? Perhaps not, perhaps yes. Once again, what if it gets covered with our names, if not photographs?

While experiencing the pain of these thoughts and embarrassing fears, I wanted to kick myself hard. Why the hell did I commit to Shankar to do this program? What fun was it? I had no one to blame because I agreed to do this of my own volition.

As I was furious with myself, I was shaken up. I almost broke my neck, not because of my anger but because our cab dashed into another vehicle due to poor visibility on the road. With heavy intensity, our cab rammed into the rear end of another cab in front, which was hardly a few feet away.

Was it a sign of my imagination turning true? Accident, news coverage, our names, Nagarjuna people reading it... oh, no! I didn't want to have such powers to turn my fiction into reality.

After a few minutes of road rage, our cab guy started again and slowly but safely dropped us at the Hotel. I had a temporary sigh of relief!

BS and I delivered the program the next day. While participants found the program valuable and enjoyable, I didn't relish the experience of delivering the program. I had no purpose that justified the guilt that I was suffering!

We travelled back to Hyderabad with my imagination of all possible embarrassing moments recurring yet again. Somehow, I reached home without an iota of happiness.

Next morning in Nagarjuna office, I had this funny feeling as if everyone that I came across was telling me that they saw me in Delhi. I knew it was stupid of me to prolong this painful imagination. But I could not stop it; the sense of guilt had no end.

In hindsight, my bosses would have been pleased to grant me permission to go and deliver a learning session at a non-competing organization. It would have been so graceful and professionally honorable that way. But I chose to hide and play smart, only to suffer from intense guilt.

Lying comes with excessive baggage of guilt! Truth is always lighter to carry than a lie, which I learnt the most painful way!

18

Do What You Think is Right

The first few days of the first job bring loads of varied emotions to everyone. It was no different for me.

The prestigious National Institute of Industrial Engineering (NITIE), located near the scenic Vihar Lake, Mumbai, offered me a career launch pad. Thanks to my guru, Dr Umasankar, I got a career break, not just a job. Given my humble background and education, joining a renowned institution like NITIE was unthinkable yet a dreamy experience. I expressed my gratitude to my guru for guiding me to apply for that job and was determined to give my best to this opportunity.

Despite my poor communication skills, I started putting my heart into the work by leveraging my domain skills. I started well, and after the first few days, I felt confident I could settle comfortably into the role. Then came a day that taught me the first hard lesson of my career!

I was fortunate to get accommodation, albeit on a shared basis, on the serene NITIE campus. We had a lovely dining facility that offered a sumptuous spread thrice a day. Honestly, that was the first time I experienced such lavish breakfast choices. As a middle-class student during my master's program, the rotis made of millets with smashed potatoes offered healthy filling to my stomach; anything beyond that was a luxury and beyond reach.

On that eventful day, when I was quietly having my breakfast, Atul and a few others joined me at the table. Atul was very talkative, and he would make the quietest of the group speak up on some pretext or the other. I, too, felt comfortable with Atul. Despite my poor English expression, Atul encouraged me in conversations, and that was one of the reasons why I always looked for opportunities to be with him.

After finishing the breakfast, I rushed towards the office at the other end of the campus as it was getting close to 9AM. Atul pulled me back and insisted I walk to the main gate with him and others. I knew what Atul and his friends were up to – they used to go for a smoke after every meal. Though I didn't smoke, I was giving them company passively.

Somehow, I could not assert myself to go to office and instead walked with Atul to the main gate. As they bought cigarettes and smoked, I just stood there with tremendous unease, as it was almost 9 AM.

That was when I had the most embarrassing moment, more than perhaps the situation warranted. The NITIE office bus passed by and entered the gate, and I made eye contact with Dr Susy Philipose, my boss, who always travelled by official transport.

As she saw me from the bus, standing next to the people smoking cigarettes leisurely, I felt awkward. I was embarrassed, terrified, and anxious. After Atul and Co. finished their smoking session, I walked back painfully to the office and entered Dr. Susy Philipose's office to sign in the register (we had that system since we didn't have any biometric systems or card readers during those days!).

I could not greet her, look at her, or avoid her.

She started the conversation by asking what I was doing at the gate at 9 a.m. I tried to present some illogical logic that Atul and co. called me, and so I went. What she said at that moment taught me a lasting lesson. She said, "Do what you think is right, not what others ask you to do."

Her statement hit me hard. I knew it was unprofessional to be late, but I still went ahead. It might have been a small event, but it did teach me a lesson about professionalism. Not that the heavens would fall; it simply did not fit into a professional character to misuse the freedom that the organization offered. Especially during the early days of one's career, before one earned any professional credibility, such silly behaviours communicate the wrong image and don't augur well! Moreover, one should not adopt such work ethic – which might become a habit! Doing what one thinks is right is the beginning of self-governance. If we are honest with ourselves, we all know what is right!

19

Masking Internal Hollowness

I was a student of Andhra Loyola College in Vijayawada, which stood out for its discipline and education standards. No one would know, but I knew what kind of struggle I had gone through during my intermediate (equivalent of 11th and 12th class) before joining Loyola. I managed to clear my Intermediate course in the first division and surprised myself. On that basis, I managed to get admission to Loyola, and during those days, it was a wow! But life was not easy for me during the Loyola days.

Every day, I had to use two modes of transport – a bicycle from home to my friend's place and a city bus from there to the college. To sustain such effort day after day, I needed a lot of motivation, which was very fragile in my case. Every time I got off the bus and walked towards the imposing Loyola College entrance gate, I had an uneasy feeling as if I was walking into an elegant prison (all the Loyalites, please pardon me, that was a genuine feeling).

Looking back to understand why I felt that way, I can now understand and articulate my problem – which I could not do during those days.

I was not able to be myself once I entered the gate; excessive discipline required that I was watchful of what I was doing and what I was speaking; bright co-students meant that I had to be more prepared, at least to match them to some extent; Loyola stood for good communication in English, which was a life-threatening challenge for me.

With such internal turmoil, I had to wear a reasonably confident look on my face and in my body language, which was not real; it was not me! Such adaptation daily made me feel like a prisoner in my own mask!

When life was so tough, the Economics subject added to the misery. Mr. Thomas was our lecturer who spoke ONLY English (he was from Kerala) and did not know a bit of my mother tongue Telugu. On top of that, my comprehension of economics from his lectures was minimal.

We had a routine of revising the previous week's lessons every week. Mr. Thomas would ask us some questions, and we were supposed to answer. If one student didn't answer, he would be required to remain standing, and the next student in the row would be asked to answer. One can imagine how embarrassing it could be to keep standing until the process ends. I used to dread that session and the entire experience.

On one such occasion, I ended up standing for not answering the question. I pretended as if I just missed to recall, but in reality, I had no clue. Soon after, my pretense of recalling the answer was exposed, and I gave up; I became the target of laughter. That means people around me figured out that I was trying to fake it. Mr. Thomas also joined the laughter, which caused me a bigger embarrassment. Before moving on to the next student, Mr. Thomas commented about the new shirt that I was wearing, "Nice color shirt, with shoulder flaps!". Another laughter followed, almost causing a sinking feeling in me.

I cursed myself for wearing a fashionable shirt. I felt embarrassed for showing off externally even though I didn't feel confident internally. I was too critical of myself and concluded that one should not show off; even if one wishes, do so only when you are prepared internally. Since then, I remained simple in my dressing and demeanor.

Even today, I firmly believe that internal hollowness cannot be covered up with external dressing up—at least, not for too long! External masking with internal hollowness does more harm to your credibility!

20

Dream & Strive

During the early days of my career, I worked as a Research Associate at the Indian Institute of Management (IIM), Ahmedabad. For a person like me who did not come from any well-known educational brands, it was a sense of pride to work for IIM; it was also a tad overwhelming! I had to work with double effort to conquer my low confidence and measure up to the expectations of the brilliant minds I was surrounded with.

While doing my bit to stay meaningful in my job, I kept noticing one routine every Friday evening or Saturday morning. Some of the senior research staff and some faculty members regularly took flights from Ahmedabad to Mumbai. No – they were not visiting their families in Mumbai. They were invited by an upcoming institute called SP Jain Institute of Management & Research, Mumbai. They travelled to teach during the weekends and returned on Sunday evenings.

For a person from a middle-class humble background, getting a job was a big deal. Here, I was witnessing people having jobs, and on top of it, they were getting invitations from other organizations. They must be super talented and have made a name for themselves to such an extent that others notice them and request their time. Fascinating!

I loved hearing every weekend who was going to Mumbai from IIM, Ahmedabad. Slowly and silently, I realized that I was nurturing the dream of being invited by SP Jain Institute one day. After all, dreams have no boundaries!

After I left IIM, Ahmedabad, I didn't think much about SP Jain Institute until 1994, when I received a call from them—under dramatic circumstances—and I happened to join them full-time as a faculty member.

Even today, I receive 'invitations' from them and others to teach. I don't know if I subconsciously nurtured the dream, and it turned out to be real or if I worked on myself to such an extent that others took note of me. Irrespective of what worked in my case, one lesson for me was to get inspired by what others achieved; learn from them and drive your way forward! Dreaming without commensurate effort leaves us in frustration! When I dream, I must strive to make my dream come true.

21

Loving People, Burning Fire

I completed my bachelor's program on a high note. Getting the university's first rank was considered a worthy achievement during those days. Soon after, I faced the familiar question of what to do next, and therefore, I started scouting for my next study options.

I was drawn to a master's course in Operations Research and Quality Control. When I enquired briefly, not many knew or heard about the course (I am referring to 1984). Still, I decided to go ahead just for the sheer novelty – I guess that was my strategy of differentiating myself in a crowded market of statistics or mathematics.

With all the excitement of a new course, I reached Kurnool, a small town in Rayalaseema, a part of Andhra Pradesh. Our university extension centre was in a rented building with meagre infrastructure—the abundant enthusiasm of our young faculty being the exception!

Our food facility was in a different rented building, which was better with decent hygiene. Then came our living accommodation, a medium-sized hall in a privately owned two-storied building.

We were four of us sharing a room; during the daytime, it was our living, drawing cum study room, and in the nights, it turned into our bedroom with mattresses spread out on the floor. Within such moderate accommodation, I used to run a tiny pantry in a corner where I made coffee or tea for all of us.

I don't know what imagery you are forming about our room; may be a decent one, a moderately clean and cozy room? Good. Let us keep it that way.

Just step out of the room. We experienced the dusty verandah beneath our feet, a foul smell from the nearby open drain, a friendly fight among pigs for garbage, and the loud curses of the old land lady and her non-stop spitting of tobacco!

Somehow, wriggle of that and walk out of the gate to see horses munching grass amidst their own dung, owners of those horses grooming themselves openly on the road, and then comes a house that everyone knows but no one speaks of: A brothel house with those ladies waiting for their customers.

We had to cross all these to go to our college or walk to our canteen – every day!

When I think of it now, I wonder how I lived there for two long years and how I pursued studies for my master's degree!

When I think of it now, I can recall several factors that made it possible. Firstly, it was the magic of four roommates bonding together, accepting each other without judging and, when necessary, correcting each other.

Then there was the old land lady, who was very rough and played foul with everyone around except four of us. She loved us as her grandchildren, respected us and listened to us. We could chide her and make her quiet. Within her meagre resources, she made sweets for us on festivals or whenever we shared our academic results. Her physical environment forever remained dirty and dusty, but her heart was all very clean and pure.

Then came the horses, their owners and the women in the brothel house. Every time we walked that path, they made way for us, they withdrew themselves into their doors and waited for us to pass; we never exchanged a single word, but they knew us as young adults doing some higher study. They respected us; they made us feel special.

Perhaps they developed an image of us, which was grand. Their acts of respect made us more responsible; we didn't know then, but I can reflect now – it was the Pygmalion effect. We were growing up to live up to their positive image of us.

I feel so proud to recall how we four grabbed the first four ranks in our batch. We didn't have grand campuses, air-conditioned hostels, hygienic food spreads or well-equipped gyms; Even if they were there, we barely could afford them.

But we had lovely people around; a deep urge within and a desperate need to complete our studies and get some employment.

Loving people around and burning fire inside are good enough to achieve what one wants to!

22

Smell of New Books

Dinner time. The entire family sat around the table to eat our humble food. It was nothing fancy, just a normal vegetarian family meal.

We have maintained this routine over the years. It keeps us together and encourages sharing through better communication. I remember this practice from my school days.

Years ago, on one such night, the dinner-time conversation turned to the new academic year. My school reopened just after the summer break. I must admit, I was not dying to return to my classes. Summer vacation was a carefree time: playing to my heart, eating snacks as I wished, travelling to nearby places to stay with my cousins, movies, parks, and games—all non-expensive yet joyful options.

Returning to school after such a wonderful summer vacation was not easy. I needed extra motivation and some push to get back to my classes, books, and homework. Of course, with new academic year, I moved up to my next standard with new syllabus.

My school insisted on buying a bundle of notebooks from the school office. My Dad paid the amount and collected the huge bunch of notebooks, ruled, double-ruled, and some plain white. Those new books created some excitement in me!! My Dad neatly wrapped those books with brown glossy paper. I pasted fancy labels on each book and wrote my name along with my subject of study.

I was eagerly waiting to open the new book and started writing something. I found an exciting reason to go to school. As I was waiting for the opportunity to inaugurate the notebooks, I opened them randomly and smelled the paper. Wow, the smell of the new book was so refreshing!

Next to buy were the textbooks. They were usually available in bookshops and were a little more expensive than the notebooks. I took the long list of textbooks prescribed for each subject and accompanied my Dad to the store. My excitement peaked this time.

While I was imagining going to a big bookshop, my Dad took me to a different shop with a huge crowd. People were falling over each other and grabbing whatever the shopkeeper was throwing at them.

It was a shop that sold used books in the second-hand market. Obviously, the price was much cheaper than the new books. This second-hand book market flourished so long as the syllabus didn't change. To my misfortune, my syllabus remained the same as for my senior batch.

My Dad handed over the long list of books to the shopkeeper, who went inside to fetch the books. I was not sure what shape the used books would be. We needed to settle for the ones that the shop had to offer. Some books would have names written all over; some pages would have some lines underlined. The worst was when the short answer questions and fill-in-the-blank exercises were already filled with answers by the previous owner of the book. That would mean I didn't have the excitement of writing my own answers and checking later. The sole advantage of such second-hand books was the price. My Dad paid the money, and I carried all the books. I could feel the steep drop in my energy. The second-hand books dampened my spirit.

We returned home and were at the dinner table. My Dad was briefing my Mom about our shopping experience. I was quietly listening. He mentioned how lucky we were to get all the books in one place and how we managed to get them at a reasonable price.

As they were chatting, I uttered something with food in my mouth. Dad could not hear what I said and asked me to repeat it. I said, "It would have been wonderful if we had bought new books and not the second-hand ones." I added, "Used books don't smell good."

As soon as my Dad heard me, he reacted very sharply, which I didn't anticipate. He said how arrogant I had become and how I didn't value money. In a strong voice, he admonished me that it didn't matter which books I bought so long as I studied well.

I could not chew the food in my mouth, swallow it, or say a word. My eyes turned moist. I felt small. I cursed myself for expressing my desire to own new books.

I abruptly got up from the dining table and went off. My Dad stopped my Mom from negotiating or pampering me at that moment.

My Dad certainly had a strong point. What mattered was how studious I was, not which books I bought. How did I miss that point? But why did my Dad get so wild? He could have simply explained to me. At that moment, I didn't understand the reason for my Dad's sharp reaction, but that episode kept haunting me over the years.

Was it intended to teach me the value of money? Was it to emphasize the need to focus on my studies, not the frills? Or was it the guilt of a middle-class parent who was not financially sound enough to buy first-hand new books? Was it the case of parents wishing to give the best to their children but, given the circumstances, find themselves helpless? Was it the case of parental dilemma whether to share the family's financial challenges with children or quietly fulfil the desires? Did all of this turn into anger towards me?

Did I aspire to smell new books without realizing the family's financial affordability? Did I not appreciate how caring my parents were in shielding me from financial troubles? Did I fail to demonstrate more maturity as a child?

There is plenty of depth in this episode to introspect and interpret. For sure, it has a profound impact on me!

23

Gaining Some, Losing You

That was not the time for me to be on the beach. I was returning from the nearby town. I was to go back to the campus where I worked. But I decided to have an unusual stop at the seaside. Walking on the sand with the midday sun hovering over me was not a pleasant experience. Still, I kept walking towards the water.

The beach was empty except for a small group of young boys playing in the water. They were all lost in their act: jumping over the water, falling over each other, punching the incoming waves, allowing the waves to take them into the sea, and running back to the shore.

Their tanned, wet bodies were shining in the hot sun. Their dark complexion was illuminating their beaming laughter.

I stood there, watching them closely. An involuntary smile appeared on my face. I guess I was just mirroring them. The glitter in their eyes was something special. That joy would not come unless it was experienced from within.

They were not conscious of my presence there. They didn't slow down seeing me. No inhibitions. No compulsions. No comparisons. No expectations. No deadlines. No bosses. No targets. Just living the moment to the fullest without chasing something.

They were relishing the breezy afternoon with a sense of liberation. They were doing what they just felt like doing. They had the pride possession of freedom.

Suddenly, a thought jolted me. Do I ever experience such freedom at my workplace? Can I do what I feel like doing, of course, responsibly? Do I have a choice? Can I exercise it? How many times have I ended up doing things that I didn't like doing? Why did I do it? How did I feel?

Why this handcuffed and imprisoned kind of feeling? When did I lose that glitter inside me? What am I trading all this for? Is it worth losing myself to get something? What is the meaning of getting something when I lose myself?

My involuntary smile disappeared. I started walking back to my vehicle. I was dragging my feet in the sand. I need to get back to work -with plenty of unanswered questions within me!

24

Stand Up to What You Believe

I started my work life early—I was hardly 22 years old when I started a job. After assisting accomplished senior professors in their research and teaching assignments for a couple of years, I quickly grabbed an opportunity to teach full-time.

I didn't have the physical or professional stature to appear as a faculty. My students' profile was hardly a few years younger than mine. I was like a young man teaching my brothers and sisters. Some came from excellent schools and colleges with impeccable English (which was my vulnerability for the first several years of my career). The onus was on me to gain my students' acceptance and minimum respect - without age, experience or grey hair - to support me.

I decided to put my heart into what I was supposed to do— teach. I had only that channel to find my feet. Luckily, it paid off. Word started going around that I taught well. It gave me so much confidence, and I was ready to shoulder more responsibilities.

My dean was smart enough to spot my enthusiasm. He assigned me the huge responsibility of compiling all the grades and announcing the final course results. It kept me on my toes and made me more accountable. I managed to do well in the first semester of the new batch. I could complete the process with zero mistakes, which greatly relieved me. I also noticed a subtle change in how my colleagues interacted with me. It looked like I gained a bit more credibility, and I was not treated as a young kid among the faculty.

The second semester brought added pressure. I was teaching an extra course in addition to managing the evaluation process. As always, I put my best effort into teaching the course. At the end of the course, exciting but indirect feedback came in, which further added to my confidence. The brightest student in the class spoke to my senior faculty colleague and said, "I thought he was too young, sir, but his style of teaching was so lucid."

Apart from teaching a course and compiling the evaluations, I was facing considerable pressure from another source, which I realized once I completed the assessment of students in my course. My dean's son was my student in the batch, and he failed my course.

As formal practice, we had a meeting with all faculty members before signing off and announcing the final results to the students. The informal practice was to show the final compilation of all grades to the Dean before the faculty meeting. This time too, I went to Dean with the same.

He browsed through all the sheets, and his special pause on his son's grades didn't skip my attention.

He looked at me with a feeble smile. Gently, in a very paternalistic tone, he advised me to relook at his son's grades in my course. I told him how careful I was and how I reviewed the answers a few times before finalizing the grades.

He insisted I take another look. I quietly left his room, reviewed his son's answer script, and went back to the Dean's office in another hour.

Dean looked at me with anticipation.

"Sir, I carefully went through the answers, and I could not add any marks. This will be his final grade, sir"

"Do you mean to say my son failed in your course?" His tone was louder, and his face was stiff.

I knew that he knew the answer, so I didn't say anything.

"Do some moderation and pull him through...He is just missing the passing grade by a few marks only."

I don't know what guts I had just after a few years in my career. I replied to him politely.

"We could surely do moderation, sir, as sometimes we do when the question paper is tough. Shall I bring this up in tomorrow's faculty meeting? If we formally decide, it will help three other students also in my course""

Dean got wild.

"What do you think of yourself? What is your age, and what is your experience? Don't try to act like a hero. I am asking you to adjust the marks only for my son. I am not asking you to make it a big issue"

"That would not be right, sir. Either we moderate the marks for all similar cases, or we leave it like that, " I said and left the Dean's room. I could imagine his face behind my back.

Dean didn't bring up the moderation issue in the faculty meeting. Everyone signed off without any change and that meant Dean's son failed in my course.

What followed that episode was a social boycott. Under Dean's instructions, people stopped talking to me in open places. My work was under scrutiny. He was waiting to catch me on the wrong foot. My leaves were denied, and my deadlines were shortened.

I was made to feel the pressure. Perhaps, it was intended to make me pay a penalty for not yielding to my boss's request. Contrary to his expectations, with every passing day, I felt stronger. Of course, I did serious introspection. I didn't feel any sense of guilt. All I did was resist manipulating the system for which I was responsible. I stood by my conviction and didn't succumb to the pressure of power.

I even discussed with my family and prepared everyone for a possible job loss. They, too, stood by me, but I didn't have to quit.

Eventually, Dean's son graduated and managed to get a job. But the soreness with Dean remained. I had a rough relationship with him for so long as I worked there.

When I look back, I must thank my Dean. This episode with him taught me what it means to stand up for what you feel is the right thing to do. It made me stronger and clarified my choice. I carried these lessons throughout my career.

Living values without fear meant going through a lot of stress but coming out as a stronger individual.

25

Am I Successful?

Am I successful? Do I know how to measure success? Am I happy with my success? Is it possible to be unhappy after the so-called success? Is it too metaphysical?

I don't think I have found any satisfying answers to these questions. So, I have decided to write down my reflections on them, hoping to discover some clarity in this process.

I came from a humble background. I started as an average student (in terms of marks), and towards the end of my formal education, I bagged university ranks. Is this a success?

At the beginning of my career, I had a horrid time communicating in English or striking up conversations with new people. I worked on my deficiency and managed to gain comfort in my English conversations, mostly with anyone (though I am not a very extroverted personality). Is this a success?

Given my humble education record, which did not have any big brands of institutions, I ended up working with many big names in my career. Is it a success?

From the days of my parents' financial struggles to educate me, I have reached a place of financial security for my family. Is this a success?

I imbibed the work ethic from my Dad and learned the value of money from my Mom. I have lived with such a work ethic most of my career; whatever I took up, I wanted to give my best. I remained honest and never indulged in any fraudulent activities in my career. I never changed myself as an individual just because I became financially secure. Is it a success—living the principles that I learned from my parents?

I made considerable contributions as part of my role in every organization that I worked with. Some of them lasted longer, some of them triggered further momentum, and some of them were acknowledged. Should I consider it a success?

As a teacher, trainer, coach, and manager, I did my part in inspiring, sharing, and motivating people to develop themselves and discover their potential. Many participants acknowledged this. Is it a success?

Two of my sons are shaping into caring individuals trying to do their bit for society while building their careers. Is it a success for me?

A quick look at these statements reveals that they are nothing out of the world. They happened to me; they can happen to anyone.

Sitting alone and listing these episodes helped me put my life and career in perspective. I need to answer if my inner conscience considers them as success. That is a personal question which doesn't have any universal answer. Speaking to myself in solitude, I defined success as getting better at what I do and living as the person I wanted to be. I need to look within to check if my conscience considers them as success; then, I can derive - rather an experience - a sense of fulfilment.

If not, I need to ask why—why not accept them as success? What is the missing piece in my definition of success? If there is a missing piece, will it take away the happiness of the success so far? Not knowing what the missing piece is and not being happy with the accomplishments thus far can make life very messy. It is important to sort things out and list down what else I need to accomplish to have a sense of success if it is not there already.

In the meantime, can I not acknowledge my success so far and strive for more? It might energize me more and reinforce my confidence.

The pursuit of these questions occupies an entire life! Irrespective of the answers to these questions, one thing is sure - success is always a moving target!

26

Cumulation of Choices

Many people sound philosophical when they say that we do not have a choice of our parents. While I agree, can I say that the rest of our life is full of choices we make?

How did I perform in academics? How studious I was? Who did I choose to be my friends? Yes, they were all my choices. Of course, there was guidance and parental hinting, but I finally made those choices. Didn't I?

I recall how I developed a fear of learning the Hindi language and, therefore, explored the possibility of avoiding that subject in my school final. My parents supported my choice, and I opted for matriculation, which did not have Hindi as a part of the syllabus.

I chose to pursue higher education in a relatively new subject called Operations Research. It was a risky choice, but I made it.

I had a mental picture of who would be a good life partner. When I met such a person, I made the choice.

I followed my colleagues who were applying for courses in the USA. But soon, I realized that I was simply mimicking them without conviction. Finally, I chose to build a career and stay near to my parents in India. Again, it was my choice!

One day, I had a brief discussion with my wife, and the next day, I decided to quit my formal corporate job to start my consulting stint. It was a big choice that I made!

I realized that when I was compelled into doing something which was of not of my choice, I was reluctant. In case, I was forced into it, I could not sustain myself. I chose to rebel or move away.

We received 'attractive' consulting offers from the world's best MNCs on a few occasions. For a small consulting firm, the money on the table was huge. But it required acting against our value system.After a brief deliberation, we decided to politely decline the offer and let go of the big money. From a business point of view, it was a foolish choice, but it was our choice.

Not all choices we make are profitable. Still, we make them. Why?

It might be my value system, my fears, my preferences, my aspirations, my capacity to take risks, and so on. At the end of the day, all choices are very personal, and they are complex to explain to others.

It is also true that some of my choices may not be appreciated by those people whose lives are interconnected with mine. So long as the people who are affected by my choices are taken into confidence, I should go by my choices.

I was fortunate to be surrounded by an eco-system that respected what I stood for and shared a similar value system, lifestyle and so on. It would have been an arduous task if people around me did not share that space with me. I see so many people who do things forever reluctantly because they are not their choice. They were forced into doing things that they never chose. It is then I realize the empowerment one feels when we can exercise our choice. But for our choices, life will feel like a drag, and it doesn't feel like our life. I always remain indebted to all those who empowered me to exercise my choices in life, even at times I erred.

Does this mean I should not do anything for others' sake? Here, too, there is a choice. If you choose to value those who ask you to do something, you will go ahead and do what they ask for. Simple things like which restaurant to go to, which dish to order, which dress to wear, which ritual to perform, and so on are easy things I do to make others happy. It is my choice to make them happy. I do not feel any big compromise. Choice-making does not mean I turn rigid and unyielding. It is living as per my higher-order preferences.

Of course, there is one thing tricky about making choices. Once we make a choice, we will not have anyone to blame for our life choices. We make them, we stand by them, and we own them. We face the consequences.

The choices we make shape us and our character! After all, life is the cumulation of what we run after.

27

Meaning Beyond Craving

Sometimes, an innocent question from a kid can turn out to be a very profound one.

My son was in primary school. One day, I was driving him to school in my small car. It was a base-model four-seater with air conditioning. Compared to my earlier car, an old model Fiat without air conditioning, the new small car was an upgrade for our family.

The roads were crowded with early-to-work professionals and early-to-school kids with their parents. At the traffic signal, I stopped the car and waited. Next to us was a big car, a Mercedes-Benz. Merc zoomed fast as soon as the traffic signal turned green and was ahead of us.

I slowly started my car and followed the bigger car. My son was looking at the Merc with curiosity. I told him that it was a very expensive car with more power. He listened to me, thought for a few seconds, and then asked me a question.

"Dad, how much does it cost?"

"It costs ten times more than our small car...it is costly".

Then came the next question.

"How many can travel in that car?"

"Comfortably four, with a bit of effort, five can travel", I replied.

"Why does it cost ten times more but carry the same number of people as our car?"

I did not feel it was a question; I found it to be a statement.

My son continued his commentary.

"With the same money, we can buy ten cars like ours, and forty people can travel...isn't it true, Dad?"

It was a fact. I understood that the kid was looking at it from a utilitarian perspective. How can I explain concepts of luxury, status, societal perception, and so on?

If we take such a utilitarian view, perhaps life will be simple. We need not work hard to earn money and satisfy many other urges because we will focus on meeting the needs, not the cravings.

Will it give more peace? How do I redefine my purpose of life, a meaning to my living, working, and earning, which are mostly linked to materialistic possessions? If not craving and earning, what else do I do with myself and my life? How do I define growth and achievement beyond the materialistic possessions? How do I elevate my sense of purpose and discover the higher-order reason for existence?

28

Two Tests to Pass

It always perplexed me how the world around us interprets things.

For example, if I did not have money to take a flight and therefore travelled by train or bus, people would say I could not afford it because I was not successful enough. If I had enough money to take a flight, yet I travelled by train, they would say I was unassuming and believed in simple living. A billionaire flying economy class makes headlines, but here I am—mostly flying economy! Who cares!

When I do not aspire to amass wealth but live a contented life, society might say I am lazy, incapable, or unambitious. But if I grow rich, amass wealth, then renounce everything, and live in obscurity, they say I am a 'rishi' (saint).

When I am a middle-class guy, consider every penny as precious, and exercise caution in spending money on electricity, cars or other luxuries, people around me may see me as a spendthrift or even judge me as too stingy or miserly. When I earned millions but still chose to be careful about spending on electricity, water or other luxuries, they say I am an environmentally conscious and responsible citizen.

We come across many more such examples. I wonder why society looks at it like this!

The insight I derived is that society wants to test us at two levels. The first test is about my capability to grow rich or achieve something. It needs proof of my ability to earn or accomplish. That is the first test to pass—the material test. Once I pass that test, society tests me on my ability to relinquish and become simple—the detachment test.

I cannot act smart and jump directly to take the detachment test, which may be seen as our incapability. It must be sequential—a material test followed by a detachment test. At what stage is my life?

29

To Trust or Not To

My tryst with trust continued many occasions. My instinct is always to see other human beings as well-intended people. I tend to listen to them, take what they say at face value, and empathize.

I noticed that my instinct for trust flows even more naturally when another person meets some of the criteria. Until then, I did not realize that such positive notions were formed in my mind. I was not judgmental, but I inclined towards them more positively if they match certain aspects.

I recall one such instance. I had one professional who applied for a role in my team. I noticed that he was well-qualified from a reputed institute (first positive), relevant experience (second positive), and down-to-earth (third positive). Finally, and more powerfully, he was in the army and served the nation for a few years (the biggest positive).

I had a positive inclination and interviewed him for the position. He cleared the panel and the process with good feedback. With the panel's recommendations coupled with my positive view of his profile, we offered him a responsible role.

With my trust in him, I listened to him, believed in what he was suggesting, and approved a few of his initiatives as well. He was very communicative and punctual in all his dealings. It was going smoothly until I woke up with an alert one morning.

Another senior person in the organization heard a whisper that this professional I trusted was involved in some financial fraud. My first reaction upon hearing this was disbelief. I instantly thought someone might be jealous of this young professional and trying to ruin his reputation. Despite my disbelief, it was upon me to clear the air.

During the day, I summoned this young professional and grilled him. To my utter shock, the whisper turned out to be true. He committed fraud and swindled money by fooling people and the system. I acted swiftly and toughly. We sacked him, confiscated his car, and sealed his laptop. It was an unceremonious exit!

While I officially dealt with it the way it was supposed to be, it took me time to come to terms with myself as an individual. I was not sure if I was shocked, disappointed, disgusted, or doubted my judgment.

Is trusting someone a bad thing? I trust someone based on my instinct. With added pedigree, my reasons to trust someone gather strength. What if I go wrong in my instincts? What if people turn out to be very different despite their pedigree?

I keep saying that trust is my instinct; living up to my trust is others' choice. Is this approach too risky? Should I doubt people until they give me reasons to trust them? Will it ever happen? Is it not disrespectful to mistrust someone?

Perhaps there is no universal answer. We derive our readiness to trust from our experiences, or is it based on our deep-rooted values?

Hmmm....I have more dilemmas related to trust than clarity!

30

Is Debt A Burden?

A middle-class Indian bachelor getting married meant a lot of preparation. My case was no different. Besides the excitement of welcoming a life partner, I felt responsible for making her comfortable in a new environment. With my humble earnings, I saved and bought some essentials for my house. I was particularly eager to buy a television because I thought it would be an excellent companion to my life partner when I went away for work. I saved and bought a colour television (yes, colour TV was a luxury for me during those days).

I was happy when my in-laws were pleased with my preparations to welcome their daughter. We were settling down in our new life, and I must say, my wife slipped into her homemaker responsibilities very quickly. Seeing how swiftly she adapted to the new role and started owning up was amazing.

Soon, we faced operational difficulties. My wife struggled to store vegetables, milk, and other perishables. We did not have a fridge at home. Our house was a bit far from the market, which meant that we could only go once or twice a week to fetch things. So, we badly needed a fridge.

I did not have enough money to buy a fridge, nor was there a credit card system or EMI luring. I am talking about the early 90s. When we inquired, we learned that a fridge costs about 8000 Indian rupees, and in my savings, I hardly had 2000 rupees. I needed at least 6 to 7 months to accumulate enough money to buy the fridge. Until then, we had to live with the operational difficulty.

While returning from work one evening, I accompanied one of my senior colleagues. He was a very caring human being and always available for any support, especially at a personal level. On our way, he enquired how we were settling into the new family life. I briefly shared how we were happily settling in and how we were exploring how to fix the operational difficulty of not having a fridge.

He immediately insisted on buying a fridge and offered a friendly loan instantly. I tried to politely push back and told him about my plan to buy after a few months. He was relentless in his push, and I had to borrow money from him and buy the fridge.

I truly appreciated his gesture of helping us. However, I felt a sense of internal discomfort, perhaps because it was my first experience borrowing money from someone. Every time I saw the fridge, I was reminded of the loan I had to repay. A sense of debt-ridden feeling! It felt like a responsibility and a burden. When I see how things have shaped up now – with credit cards, loans, EMIs being the norm, I wonder why I felt the way I did during those days. Perhaps, *pleasure now—pay later* was not for me!

Perhaps it was a supreme degree of self-respect, and borrowing money was damaging it internally. Or perhaps I wanted to stand on my feet and not depend upon others to lead my married life.

My wife and I discussed and decided to be very frugal for the next few months. We saved every rupee and repaid the money well before six months. We felt liberated, so we had some chilled water from the fridge and watched colour television—with a great sense of satisfaction and contentment!

I realized that I prefer living within my means and feeling lighter! More importantly, when I carry no debt, I retain the liberty to exercise choices in my life. No compulsive living because I am debt-ridden!

31

Have A Friend, Be Yourself

During the early part of my career, I moved away from my family and had to stay alone in Mumbai. During the week, work kept me busy. On many occasions, I chose to stay late at work so that I could directly go for dinner before hitting the bed. It was that time when the TV in the room was a luxury and there was no concept of mobile phones. If I reflect now, I wonder how we could live without a TV in the room and mobile in the hand!

Honestly, it felt very lonely to go home early from work. Without family at home, my only companion was a book or Panasonic cassette player, until I fell asleep.

In such a situation, the weekend was the most dreaded time. After a lazy morning and late breakfast, I did not know what to do for the rest of the day. The city was new; I knew no one other than my work colleagues. How nice would it be to have someone I could go to and be myself with?

Fortunately, I have one such friend, Suri. He was my classmate and roommate during my college days. It was a pleasant coincidence that he was in Mumbai the same time that I was working in the same city.

With him around, my weekends turned out exciting, something I could look forward to. I experienced the joy of having a friend who met me on most weekends. Suri used to travel a long distance to reach my place and then take me around the city. We travelled economically in a local train, reached some prominent places, browsed through the books on the pavements, bought cheap T-shirts, ate at inexpensive food joints, and watched movies.

With him on my side, the dreaded weekends were the most joyful days. What made it so joyful was that I did not have to condition myself or project myself. I was just being myself without any pretence. I was not claustrophobic; I accepted my vulnerabilities of not knowing the place or the local language; there was no hesitation; I liked my dependency on him.

After a full day outing with Suri, my happy soul and tired body effortlessly slipped into sleep. Even today, if I visit Mumbai and have some time to catch up, I do meet Suri and spend some quality time.

True friendship means offering quality time, listening unconditionally, and accepting the person without judgment! Having at least one such friend in your life is a blessing.

32

Be Pragmatic, Not Just Idealistic

It is common to receive feedback, suggestions, advice, or help to improve ourselves. Feedback is one of the most important contributors to our growth as people and professionals. One must be open to receiving and processing such input, especially when it comes from a credible person that you trust.

I, too, received many such inputs and processed them at my discretion. One of the comments was very sticky; it made me think a lot and calibrate my beliefs. It stayed with me for a very long time and continues to cross my thoughts from time to time.

Several years ago, I worked very closely with one of the CEOs. He has high standards, principles, long-term thinking, and a bigger vision. Working with him elevated my thinking and allowed me to learn faster. The best part of the CEO was his openness to discussion if we engaged him in quality conversations.

I was always excited to have deep conversations with him. Before every such occasion, I read a lot, gathered best practices, and proposed many ideas. The CEO approved some of them with a few suggestions, and the going was good.

With every nod from him, I could see progress during the ideation and conceptualization phase. The experience started altering when the ideas entered the implementation phase.

People in the organization had different views on the importance of what was proposed. Some had different ways of doing things. They also had some personal agendas that did not go well with what we were proposing. I believed that their resistance was not merely based on merit; it had ulterior motives. It was slowing me down. At times, I had to compromise and do something suboptimal just to keep people happy.

After a few months, I had a chance to discuss the overall progress with the CEO. Given my comfort with him, I opened myself up and shared my thoughts with a touch of frustration.

Why could not people see what was good for the organization? Why did they bring in their personal interests? Why could not they elevate their thinking? Had they been like-minded, we would have made much more progress.

I noticed how the CEO was listening to my pouring out. He had a gentle smile which communicated that he understood me, empathized with me and at the same time, he had his own wisdom.

With his soft voice, he said, "You must be more pragmatic than idealistic".

It was short and straight. I mentally noted his statement and left the CEO's office. His simple suggestion kept ringing in my mind. I referred to the dictionary to confirm my understanding of the word 'pragmatic' – dealing with problems with a touch of practicality rather than a set of principles.

It took some time to comprehend my CEO's suggestion. I had to deal with some of my internal dilemmas. I had a doubt if pragmatic meant compromising my values and principles; does it mean diluting my ideals? Should I give up just because others have their agenda and my ideals do not suit them? For a moment I thought being a leader means sticking to what you believe and convincing others to come along.

I played and replayed the statement – be more pragmatic than idealistic. Slowly but surely, I developed my own clarity.

> First, I need to figure out what values, principles, and ideals I truly and deeply believe in.

> Next, I need to be practical to implement the same. It does not mean I give up my values or ideals; instead, I find a way of implementing them with persuasion and pursuance with perseverance and patience.

I also understood that every idea need not be an ideal and I should not be rigid about the same; I should be open to receiving new ideas and approaches from others so long as they do not conflict with my ideals.

Sticking to my core and at the same time, valuing diversity is at the heart of the pragmatic approach suggested by my CEO!

33

Sequential Vs Parallel Thinking

Thinking about how I think is a great reflective exercise! Over the years, I realized one big shift that I needed in the way I think.

Early in my career, I was a sequential thinker, meaning I could focus and think on one task or one responsibility at a time. My belief was that to get good-quality output, I had to concentrate all my energies on one thing. I feared poor results and reduced intensity if I split my thinking on more than one thing at a time. But I had to change.

I do not say that focusing on one thing at a time is entirely wrong. However, the roles I was asked to play required me to handle multiple responsibilities on a given day. I could not insist that I would accept one after the other. I realized that work environments or roles we play in life do not support such sequential thinking. They expected me to manage myself and learn to handle diverse things.

It was not easy for me to break my habit of sequential thinking. First, I accepted that I had to perform more than one responsibility on a given day or during a specific time. It was up to me to allocate my mind space and manage my focus.

I would not say I was multitasking, but I surely managed to spread my wings and switch between many tasks. I practised jumping from one task to another and remained focused on one task at a time.

It required disciplining my mind and properly allocating mind space to different responsibilities that were running concurrently. It called for quickly retrieving the necessary information about the task and continuing from where it was left. It needed managing emotions while switching between the tasks. It led me to deft role-playing in terms of my behaviours and skills as per the responsibility on hand.

While keeping multiple responsibilities on my mental radar, I started to focus intensely on one task at a time. With this switching capability, I came out of sequential thinking and became a parallel thinker without compromising on my intensity or quality. Many on mind, but one in hand!

34

Thankless Feeling

At workplaces, we often hear comments like "Mine is a thankless job!". Well, people tend to be more vocal about workplaces. However, as we think of our roles in life, there are many occasions when we would have felt the same. It is quite possible that we did something to someone, and they never bothered to turn back and express their gratitude. How do you deal with such a feeling of being 'used' by someone?

With such a sense of hurt, we relate more closely whenever we see a doormat or tissue paper. We might feel that someone exploited us and threw us away.

I, too, had similar feelings during some phases of my life. I would have extended some moral support, offered some advice, supported them financially, or helped them with career planning. They would have benefitted and progressed. But then they moved on and never bothered to thank me. I felt used, ignored, or taken advantage of. It surely felt bad.

After a few such occasions, I paused and asked myself the question: "How many people have helped me in my life so far and how many times have I expressed my gratitude?"

It was a powerful mirroring question. I realized that there were several impactful people in my personal and professional life. I thanked some of them, while I remember several others in my heart, but never expressed explicitly!

I summarized my insight in one line:

When you express gratitude, you feel light and happy; when you expect gratitude, it may cause anxiety or disappointment.

Since then, my outlook has been to do my bit if it helps others. The joy of doing my bit itself is my reward; beyond that, I never expect anything in return. If they look back to thank me, I take it as a bonus!

When others 'use' me, the more significant take away is that I am useful to someone. This perspective liberates me and gives so much meaning to my life!

35

Lessons From Opportunities

Missing some opportunities when they knock on our door is a common experience in most lives. The same has been true in my life, too. In my nostalgic moments, I recall some of those interesting episodes.

***

Very early in my life, I missed one opportunity to act as a child artist in a movie. My classmate Sridhar was a rich kid; we attended some tuition classes together. He developed a strong bond with our family, and on some occasions, he preferred to stay at our place overnight. He felt at home!

He once told me that a film was being shot at his palatial residence, and the house was in a mess. I was curious to see how a film was shot and asked him to take me to his place one day.

On that eventful day, Sridhar came to the tuition class but didn't find me there. He then went to my house and found the door locked.

I was out with family for a function and did not inform him (we did not have mobiles, landlines, or WhatsApp during my childhood).

Two days later, I met Sridhar at the tuition class. He was so upset and fumed at me. The reason was that he missed taking me home to act in that film. I learnt that the film crew that day was discussing a scene and wanted to urgently look for a child artist to act as the hero's son. When Sridhar heard this conversation, he quickly jumped in and promised to get me in a few hours. When he could not get me, the crew managed the scene with someone else.

Sridhar felt terrible that he could not see his friend debuting in films.

Had I acted in that film, I might have grown in that career and become a star—who knows!

I learnt one thing: I should never mind one lost opportunity because it might be my opportunity to explore the other aspects of myself.

***

Another lost opportunity was to join a huge public sector organization and grow in my career.

In my first job, I was a research associate attached to a professor. As part of the job, I had to make a presentation that was attended by many other professors. I completed my first presentation with heavy preparation and felt relieved.

A day after my presentation, another senior professor caught up with me in the dining hall and started striking a conversation. It was the first time I met him, and I noticed how he tried to make me comfortable by adding a personal touch to the conversation. He concluded the discussion with an invite to visit his house – which was on campus – for lunch. It was a rapid development, and the introvert in me could not imagine going to his place for lunch. I kept the invitation in abeyance.

A few weeks passed, and the senior professor bumped into me in the corridors and insisted I come for lunch. With great reluctance, I went to his place on a Sunday. It was a tough one hour to engage with him. During this hour, I was briefly introduced to his daughter, who came into the dining hall for a minute.

There was silence for a few days, and the senior professor called me to his office.

He asked me to join a huge public sector organization where he had deep connections. He kept counselling me, saying great things about the large public sector organization and how I could grow to become a director.

After a long conversation, I requested him to tell me how to apply. He then revealed his mind.

"Don't worry about applying; when I visit them next time, I will put a word, and they will call you for an interview. It is just a formality", he said.

While the job was very promising, I wouldn't say I liked the channel of getting that job. Perhaps, I wanted to earn that opportunity on my merit, not through his recommendation or influence. I reluctantly nodded my head. He then continued.

"In fact, I desire to see you join that organization and get married to my only daughter; your career and life will be completely set!"

I was stunned. I got perplexed and struggled to hide my expressions.

Was it a quid pro quo? Should I marry his daughter to get a secure job in a large organization? I did not pursue either of them - neither the job nor the daughter. Honestly, I did not like the overall spirit.

I left his place and remained silent. Imagine how awkward my situation would have been on the office campus until I left that organization. I avoided encountering the senior professor, though I occasionally saw him in some official gatherings. I could see how he chose to ignore me.

I do not know if I missed some huge opportunity in life, but I have learnt one important insight: *sometimes, opportunities come to test our character*. By saying no to some of them, we strengthen ourselves.

36

Create Your Happy World

We are all in search of happiness, though we know it is always a passing cloud and a fleeting feeling.

Some of us make our happiness contingent upon possessions or achievements. For example, I will be happy the day I own a house. When I upgrade my car, I will be happy. When I earn so much, I will be happy. All these events can happen, give us some happy feeling and then they move on.

I had similar thoughts. I didn't know how to differentiate between success and happiness, and I was also not sure if every success gave me happiness. But I did feel joyful at that moment of some achievement or possession, and then life took me to other events.

While I continue my exploration of happiness, in recent years, I have observed myself and reflected on a different question: What helps me to be myself, and which environment makes me enjoy my journey irrespective of success? It need not be an accomplishment or possession that makes me happy. It could be a moment, the environment, people, or a small gesture. They could be my source of happiness.

During my travels, whether on flights, long car rides, or long waits in traffic jams, I replayed many instances and recalled how each situation made me feel. My attempt was to find a pattern in the way I felt in various circumstances and with diverse people.

Hurray, I could find some patterns within myself!

I realized that I was most comfortable, behaved naturally, and experienced joy whenever I had people who were genuine, authentic, humble, and respectful towards others. They were not self-obsessed or double-faced, nor did they project themselves to be superior creatures. Such people put me at ease and allowed me to be myself.

Another pattern I noticed was how a negative environment upsets me and destroys my happiness. Any negative talk, gossip, talking ill about someone, cut-throat winning attitude even through dubious means, always doubting people, recalling the past, regretting the choices, blaming someone, jealousy...any of these actions sapped my energy. At times, they made me lose my balance and get angry.

Instead, if the environment is trusting and I am surrounded with well-meaning people, any amount of hard work does not upset me. When placed in such positive surroundings, I am ready to experiment even if success is not guaranteed.

If I analyse deeper, I am sure I will understand myself and my source of happiness even more. For now, I chose two specific actions for myself:

1. Watch and decide who I wish to build and nurture a relationship or association with

2. Influence the environment to discourage negativity and, instead, engage in solution-seeking pursuit.

Through these intentional efforts, I can create a world where I can be myself! That is a happy world for me.

37

Impress A Select Few

Early in my life and career, I realized that we live in a society where impressing others has become a norm. From a young age, we were told to dress well, speak politely, extend courtesies, be nice and achieve things to impress others, let it be good grades in school, admission into good colleges or entry into a career with security and fat salary.

But the rebel in me – just as in most people – kept questioning: why impressing others is given so much importance? Is it essential? Does it help us in any way? And most importantly, what happens when we try to impress others or fail to impress?

While impressing others may seem like a harmless pursuit, I realized that the pressure to maintain an impressive image was exhausting and taking me away from my real self. I felt as if I was wearing a mask and operating to impress others. I felt the strong urge to remove the mask, liberate myself and feel lighter.

Fortunately, before I jumped to a conclusion, I realized that this phenomenon of impressing others has deeper insights. While impressing others by behaving according to their expectations cannot be the sole purpose of life, I understood that it was also important for me to live up to the expectations of some people I truly care for and respect. It offers a lever for my upliftment.

My first positive attempt to impress was when I referred to many books and picked up challenging problems to solve during my master's course. My teacher, Dr KVS Sarma, was impressed. During my stint at the Indian Institute of Management (IIM), Ahmedabad, I tried to impress Professor Arvind Tripathy by preparing course material with thorough research. His appreciation of 'my touch' to the overall output lifted my confidence. I worked hard several times to impress my participants in most of my training programs and workshops. All these attempts consumed a lot of my energy, but I realized that I was growing in the process of impressing others.

While making a good impression has its benefits in certain situations, I experienced that constantly seeking validation from others and the need to impress them was not worth sacrificing my authenticity. On some occasions, when everyone around me was trying to impress the bosses or seniors with their flattery, I struggled. I chose to avoid such encounters or remained silent in those moments. In all such situations, remaining true to myself and not trying to impress others superficially was a lot of effort.

In due course, I told myself that the most important person to impress is myself. With this insight, I developed a thought clarity that I need not stretch to impress all; instead, I should make a choice of people that I want to impress so that I lift myself and grow as a person. That will impress me as well!

38

Fear: Friend or Foe?

Fear is an interesting emotion that plays an important role in many lives. Mine is no different. I keep reminiscing about some of those occasions in my life to understand if fear has been my friend or a foe!!

My early memory of fear and how it impacted my behaviour was that of a language class in my high school. We had a Hindi language class twice or thrice a week - the one I used to dread the most. For some reason, I am poor at picking up languages. Perhaps, I didn't catch the trick of building linguistic capabilities in me. On top of it, my Hindi teacher turned out to be a ruthless person with a smile. I vividly recall - that smile was a combination of sarcasm and sadism. His punishments were very much DIY - I had to raise my arm, keep my palm upside and hit my finger knuckles against the table. My teacher should hear the sound of knuckles hitting the table, while he was sitting in his chair at a distance.

Every time I realized that we had a Hindi class on the schedule for the day, a shiver passed through my spine.

My hands sweated, and my smile disappeared. All signs of fear engulfed me. My instinct was to skip going to school and thereby avoid Hindi class. This was not a possible option because Hindi was staggered across the week. Somehow, I gathered courage and dragged myself to the school.

As we got closer to the Hindi class, courage was replaced with intense fear - fear of punishment, fear of humiliation, fear of feeling small, and fear of feeling inadequate. I froze and lost even the bit that I prepared during my homework. I failed again. And I was punished again. It was getting obvious to me that I would never be able to pick up Hindi language.

When I think of it now, my fear of the teacher turned into a dislike for the language. That was a huge mistake!! My mental block towards Hindi remains with me even now!

***

Fear held me back another time. During the early days of moving away from home, life offered a new experience—living independently, travelling alone, and spending money as I wished without immediate monitoring. Newly found freedom can get very intoxicating. It prompted me to try a few things that I had never done earlier: going to consecutive movie shows, eating out, and, on one occasion, wanting to try smoking a cigarette!

Despite the new urge to smoke, I didn't want to do it with my classmates or roommates for fear of losing my image with them. They often thought I was a very studious student with a lot of discipline. Fear held me back!

On one occasion, I was alone, travelling overnight by bus. We stopped enroute for a short break. Passengers jumped out, had a cup of tea in the cold winter weather, and some lit a cigarette as well. That was the moment which ignited my urge!

I bought one cigarette, lit it and put it between my lips to grab a puff. Every bit of my action was so amateurish - struggling to cover up before others noticed me as a first-time smoker.

After the first few puffs, a fear of being watched surfaced. What if someone I know sees me? What if they carry this news to my parents or classmates? Will I be questioned? Will I be pulled up? With this fear, I moved to the darker side, away from the light and continued with a couple more puffs.

The whole visual of me with a cigarette in hand, hiding in the dark, away from the crowd and with the lurking fear in me didn't please me at all. In one flash, I threw the cigarette away, started chewing some mouth freshener and walked into the light. The sense of liberation I experienced at that moment was like a fresh breeze...

very light and pleasant with fragrance. I thanked my fear of getting exposed for pulling me out of darkness - literally!! That was an occasion where my fear became my conscious keeper and made me do what made me feel comfortable.

Since then, I have realized that fear has a very beneficial side, and I must respect it!

39

Zone of Calmness

At our workplaces, we interact with many colleagues, and everyone forms certain opinions about us. Some share with us, while some talk about us behind our backs. On one occasion, fortunately for me, I had a lady colleague who commented and posed a question straight to me: "You look very calm and pleasant most of the time; is it really you, or are you putting up a face?"

Well, I received the comment with a smile, though I did not know how to convince the lady that I was not faking my calmness.

But I kept thinking - how is it that I do not get rattled or look disturbed? Well, at least most of the time. Is it because I think more and worry less?

As I kept reflecting, I developed more clarity in thinking against worrying. They are two different zones.

I realized that when I engage in thinking, I acknowledge the task or problem, analyze, reflect, and make decisions. On the other hand, I noticed that worrying pushes me into a form of negative thinking that is often fuelled by anxiety or fear. It creates imaginary fears or uncertainties without actively seeking solutions or making decisions. On those occasions of worry, I look grim and low on energy. I, therefore, consciously kept working on myself to minimize those episodes of worry by detecting them quickly.

Missed opportunities, new demands from clients, monetary losses, complex issues at workplace...any such episodes triggered more of my thinking.

On most occasions, I retain the locus of control by consciously activating the thinking faculty within me. This approach helps me explore possible courses of action instead of passively worrying. Perhaps that is the critical factor for my calm demeanour.

Having said that, I also noticed another pattern in my worry.

When people that I trust cheat on me, I slip into worry. When people I groomed surprise me with their arrogance or irresponsibility, I worry. It is a bigger worry when I need to continue my association with people with a conflicting value system. Luckily, these are more exceptions and are not regular occurrences.

So long as I operate in my thinking zone, I remain calm. Thank you, lady, for prompting me to explore the secret of my calmness!

40

Aspire With Contentment

One reflection that my wife and I fondly relive very often is how we are contented with 4k or 400k the same way.

Early in our marriage, I earned 4k monthly salary, of which around 10% was deducted towards the official accommodation provided to us. We were blessed not to have any financial responsibility towards anyone else in our family other than taking care of us both. This helped us plan our expenses more predictably.

While we were undoubtedly frugal, we never compromised on the simple joys of married life. We regularly went out every weekend, watched movies, ate out and bought household things. We managed to buy a colour television (though small in size), a gearless scooter (quite a trend during those days) and some cane furniture (which was functional but not expensive) for our living room. We never felt any sense of scarcity. We never felt deprived.

Things have not changed dramatically, even today, when my earnings crossed 400k. Our lifestyle is the same, and our joys are the same. More money never meant more joy because less money was not causing less joy.

My wife reminisces with a sense of satisfaction about how happy we were then and how happy we are now. This experience helped us realize that the secret of our happiness is contentment and alignment.

We learnt to live happily with what we have, instead of making our happiness contingent upon something else. We never told ourselves that our lives would be better if we moved into a bigger house or bought a better car. We have been happy with what we have and what we have been getting.

Does it mean that we were lazy? No. Contentment does not mean that we become inactive or complacent. While experiencing contentment with what we have, we kept striving towards more wealth and a secure future. We derived a complex insight into how we need to pursue aspirations while experiencing joy with what we have.

The second critical factor we realized was our alignment. My wife and I share a common outlook on money. Money is important in life, but it is not the only thing to chase. Money should not influence who we are fundamentally. We experienced how crucial such alignment is for happiness.

When there is no alignment, our goals will differ. There will be mutual pressures to pursue different things, which will take life in different directions. If one feels that joy lies in buying a four-bedroom house by taking a loan, and if the other thinks that a two-bedroom apartment without any debt is much better, then there are differences in pursuit and there is no happiness.

Similarly, our parents and siblings never placed their expectations on us or tried to influence our lifestyle. My wife and I stayed aligned without any comparisons with others.

After more than thirty years of togetherness, we were reinforced that happiness is a choice and not a dependent variable. Of course, it must be a shared choice of the family! That makes life even more peaceful.

Cursed My Mom, But Loved!

Did you ever curse your Mom? I did.

Soon after I started my career with a meagre salary, my mother forced me to do something I did not like.

After getting my first job, I moved to a different city. I received my salary for a few months before I travelled home to spend some time with my parents. I shopped for a saree and shirt for my parents and some items for my sister. With a sense of pride in gifting them something with my own earnings, I reached home. They, too, were pleased with my gesture.

We had a lovely family time, watching movies and eating good food. One evening, a guest dropped in. I did not know who he was until my Mom told me that he was her professional acquaintance. I formally greeted him when my mother introduced me to him.

I was perplexed when he did not stop with pleasantries. Instead, he kept probing me about my date of birth, salary and expenses. I felt uncomfortable as I did not understand the context.

My Mom chipped in, saying that she called him home to enrol me into a life insurance policy. Her idea was that I should start a policy because I started earning. I got furious. It was not because my Mom did not tell me before; I hated it because I did not want to commit myself to a long-term premium-paying burden while I was still finding my feet in my first job.

Perhaps I wanted to have liberty with my earnings without being bound by this financial commitment of paying the premium without fail. I tried to push back and postpone.

But my Mom and the insurance agent were very persistent. I succumbed to the pressure, but I hated my Mom for pushing me into this. With huge resistance, I took the bare minimum commitment for 25 years. Though my mother did not appreciate the lower insurance coverage, she let me go with it, perhaps thinking we had made a beginning, at least.

After 25 years, I received a call from the insurance company informing me that my policy had matured. They wanted me to furnish my bank details so that they could transfer the full amount on maturity.

When I saw the amount credited to my bank account, I recalled the day I reluctantly started my insurance policy. As I continued growing in my career, the small premium amount never bothered me much, though it all accumulated into a substantial amount.

When I saved drop by drop, it turned into a pot full!

When I read the writings of financial advisers these days, they all say, 'Start saving early and see the magic of compounding.' I am fortunate to have had my mother as my financial advisor early in my life, much before experts came onto the scene! Thank you, Mom, for pushing me into this habit of saving, which has given me so much financial security in life!

42

Choose Worthy Conflicts

Conflict is usually not my cup of tea.

But I did, and I do find myself in conflicting situations. Life experiences made me realize that life cannot be like a feel-good Indian movie with melody songs and scenic visuals without a villain.

Over the years, I reasoned that I need not deal with all conflicts; some conflicts go away by simply accepting things as they are. For example, at the workplace, my working style may differ from that of my colleagues. We end up in a conflict if I am forced to change or I force my colleague to change. Instead, if I accept that my colleague's working style is different, but we are working for the same result, I make peace with myself. Similarly, at home, my family may not have the same entertainment tastes. I may like songs, but my spouse may like devotional videos. So long as we don't force each other to develop similar tastes, we are good. So, there are some conflicts that are not worth resolving; it is better to accept diversity. Honestly, it took a while to develop this perspective.

On the other hand, I find myself at odds with dealing with internal conflict in some situations. These conflicts arise out of value differences. If I value quality and my business partner values money, then we are in conflict, and I cannot simply accept. With this inner turmoil, I came to understand that there are some areas where I take a hard stand and cannot compromise. That results in a conflict.

I encountered conflicts in my work on a few occasions that I could not easily brush aside. This created a lot of internal chatter because on one end, it was my value system, and on the other end, it was my seniors or relationships. Should I express my disagreement? Should I refuse to do what I did not feel comfortable with? Should I escalate and instigate office dynamics? What would be the repercussions if I did anything or nothing?

It was difficult for me because conflict was not my cup of tea. It resulted in many sleepless nights. In most such situations, the only way I dealt with such value conflicts was to voice them directly or use passive responses and body language. I waited to see if things would change to my liking. If not, I excused myself from such assignments or tasks, which certainly angered my seniors, and I faced their ire and stood by my beliefs. The important thing for me in such circumstances was to be prepared mentally to face the extreme consequences, such as losing my job or relationship.

I traded the security of my job to preserve my value system. It caused some stress and tension in the short term but made me stronger in the long run.

Overall, I realized that conflicts are plenty; but I need to choose those conflicts that are worthy to deal with.

43

Survive or Stand Up?

It was a bright Monday morning when my new boss, Rohil, summoned me into his office. His face was beaming with enthusiasm, and I guessed some weekend spark must have struck him. Rohil was a very young second-generation businessman. I was assigned to his team of new start-ups.

"We need fresh talent. Let us hire from top institutes," he declared, his voice charged with excitement. "I want you to find the brightest young minds and bring them on board."

His sudden shift in demeanour was suspicious, and I was apprehensive about the sustainability of this enthusiasm.

Nevertheless, I contacted universities over the next few weeks and created enough interest in campus hiring. Selling the start-up idea, which was present only in Rohil's mind and didn't exist in any tangible form, was challenging.

Rohil and I travelled to those campuses; we met some incredibly talented young individuals, full of potential and eager to make their mark. Selling the start-up idea was my responsibility, while Rohil chose the candidates. At the end of the process, I felt a sense of accomplishment as I could convince and get the bright talent into our company.

Each new hire brought a fresh wave of energy and excitement. The old timers from the other business divisions turned their heads to look at these young people walking in the corridors and cafeteria. It felt as if we were on the verge of something great.

However, things took a drastic turn just a month into their tenure.

Rohil called me for an emergency meeting. As I entered the conference room, I saw Rohil seriously working on his computer, but he did not look into my eyes. I suspected something untoward was hitting me.

"We've had a change of plans," Rohil spoke sternly. "The new hires are no longer needed. You can send them off".

My heart sank. I was the face of the company for these young stars, and now I had to deliver the crushing news. I did not enjoy any great rapport to argue with Rohil.

The days that followed were the hardest of my career. I saw the disappointment and confusion in the eyes of those I had fought so hard to bring in. Each conversation was a dagger to my conscience. Knowing that these decisions could derail their budding careers, I felt terrible for being the bearer of such news. My respect for myself and my role was slipping through my fingers.

Frustration and anger bubbled within me. I wanted to storm into Rohil's office, demand an explanation, and perhaps even hand in my resignation.

But the thought of my family and necessity of a job held me back. Moreover, I felt my resignation would be cowardly and did not want to run away.

Over the next few days, I was torn between my principles and the practicalities of life. Should I survive or stand up? What should I do? I didn't know exactly, but I had to do something.

My ever-supportive spouse reminded me of my strength and encouraged me to stand up for what I believed in and consider the broader picture.

After a few days, I decided to take a step. I requested a private meeting with Rohil's dad, the business group's chairman. My heart pounded as I walked into his office, determined yet nervous.

I was about to speak negatively about his son with a business owner. What if he wouldn't like to hear what I said and what if he sacked me? Well, I was mentally ready for the extreme measure. I wanted to act and feel right.

I began, my voice steady but firm. I expressed my concerns about the ethical distress I experienced and the potential damage to the company's reputation.

His reaction was measured and balanced. He understood my view and obliged my request to shift me to another division away from Rohil.

Rohil was furious and arrogantly asked me to leave his start-up venture. I left his office but continued in the company for a few more years.

The entire experience left an indelible mark on my career. It taught me the value of standing up for what is right, even facing daunting challenges. It reinforced the importance of empathy and the impact of our decisions on others' lives. And most importantly, it reminded me that in the whirlwind of decisions, staying true to one's principles is the anchor that keeps me grounded.

Of course, I still feel guilty for what I did with that young talent. I could not stop the unfair treatment meted out to them. Or was it a blessing in disguise that I saved them from Rohil sooner?

44

Don't Compare Me!

One statement that I always hated from my Mom was, "Look at Gopal; how much household work he does."

Whenever my Mom said something like that, I usually had a very sharp reaction. I usually became adamant about not doing what my Mom was expecting me to do. I expressed my displeasure at hearing about Gopal—who was just a neighbour's kid of my age. I made it a point to push back stubbornly and refused to change. Why was I behaving the way I did?

As I grew up, I realized that I was not angry with my Mom or I was not hateful towards Gopal. It was my dislike of comparisons that manifested as anger or rigidity.

What is wrong with comparisons? We see it as the usual trick to provoke or motivate someone to up their game. By quoting one person's behaviour, we intend to inspire another. The expected outcome is seeing the second person stepping up to match or surpass the first person. Though the intention was to push me up, why was it not working on me?

A more profound thought offered me an insight. It was not that I was not ready to be compared, but who you compare me with mattered to me. I suppose Gopal was not the person that I wanted to be compared with. On certain aspects of household work, he might be better. But overall, on many other aspects, I might have considered myself to be better than Gopal. Perhaps my ego did not accept Gopal as a benchmark for me. So, I hated such comparisons.

On a different track, when people compared my amateur singing with that of the legendary singer Dr SP Balasubramanyam (SPB), I did not feel bad. I listened to my song and was comparing myself with SPB, though I knew I needed to improve a million more times to be any match to that blessed artist. How was I so open to comparisons?

My self-realization is that when you want to pep me up to do better, use really high benchmarks. Comparing me with peers who are almost like me might hurt my ego, which will trigger more rebellious responses and rejection than improvement. Unwittingly, I might start hating the person that you are comparing me with, though it has nothing to do with that person.

This reflection helps me understand sibling rivalry within families or a competitive attitude among colleagues at work. Such acts of comparison do not promote collaboration. Set more inspiring benchmarks or stroke the inner compass of the individual; they have better chances of triggering improvements.

45

Value Me, Not the Brand I Wear

In many other places in this book, I described my humble beginnings and how my circumstances, parents and their upbringing shaped me. Our economic status did not allow me to wear branded clothes early in my life. I did not nurture any ambition of going to premier institutes either. I did not fancy buying things that were not needed. Perhaps, I could not afford any of them during those days.

There is a popular quote: " Never say you cannot afford it. That is a poor man's attitude. Instead, ask how you can afford it." Going by this saying, I should have worked hard to earn more, so that I could afford all the big brands and luxuries. But I had a contrarian view.

Why do I need to wear a brand? Does the brand of my pen improve the quality of my writing? Does the brand of my watch help me decide the time of the day? The answer is a clear no.

Or do people respect me more based on the brand I wear? If so, do I need the respect of those who look at the brand that I use more than the person that I am?

With all this chatter in my mind, it was becoming clear that I had two options: either I earn so much more that I can afford bigger brands, or I need to become a brand on my own. Well, I chose the latter.

My choice may sound a bit arrogant, but it was more pragmatic. By the time I analysed people's responses, I had completed my master's and was pursuing my doctoral program—not from a branded university again. Practically, I did not have a chance to go back in time and add brands to my educational qualifications. My only choice was to move ahead and make a career. Therefore, I wanted to build my own brand through my actions.

How to build a personal brand? I had no clue. I only believe that our body of work creates our professional brand. I put in effort from my heart in every opportunity that came my way. I attempted to get rid of all my pretences as soon as I realized them. I had this urge to meet the expectations of those I greatly respected and placed them very high in mind. I was eager to impress the people that I respected. That zeal to get appreciation from those people was a big driver that made me perform and helped me create a track record, which helped me build my credibility.

When people start respecting you for what you are and not merely based on the car you came in or the mobile phone you use, you know you are beyond wearable brands. Building such standing is harder work than buying a branded item, but that is the challenge I relished! And I truly believe that the impact of such an effort lasts longer!

How big a brand have I become? No, I never got into that debate with myself. After all, it is all relative.

46

God – When I Need

During my schooling, the final examination season was always stressful. The announcement of the exam schedule always triggered my stress.

Self-doubt in my preparation, coupled with fear of failure, was a killer combination that played havoc with me. I could not eat my food peacefully, spend time with visitors who came home, didn't feel like getting out of bed in the morning, or sleep calmly at night. Watching movies was temporarily banned, but newspapers advertised the upcoming movies very tantalisingly. In the middle of all of this, some subjects troubled me endlessly.

Parents provided the resources and motivation, and teachers taught the subjects as best they could. However, I still felt inadequate and needed help to get through exam season!

Oh, God...please help me!

Come the exam season, the religious God-fearing personality revealed itself from within. Weekly or sometimes daily (if the fear was more intense) visits to the nearby Hanuman temple became a norm.

Having darshan of the powerful God, praying, and doing eleven rounds around the temple (pradakshina) were rituals that offered a lot of psychological strength. My studiousness, coupled with a strong belief that God was behind me, helped me pass the exam season with flying colours.

This practice continued until my last formal education. Whatever my place of study, I spotted the nearest Hanuman temple and followed the same ritual during the exam season.

What would be God's impression of me? He would have felt that I was an opportunist who approached him only when I badly needed strength. My behaviour was exactly like that – remembering, visiting and praying in times of stress and low confidence. Was it opportunistic?

I did not think so. I never believed that God always wants us to rely on him. I do not think God would be proud of his creation to be always dependent on him. If God were to be like my parents or teachers, He would feel happy that I operate mostly on my own and approach Him when I badly need help.

To me, God is always available on call whenever I am in distress. God is the power to augment my psychological strength, which enables me to face any challenges of life. I do not shy away from giving a shout-out and asking for His help!

47

My Parents Parenting

In my observation, every child's relationship with its parents has a different flavour. Some relationships are dominant with pampering, some with controlling, some with indifference, and some with mistrust. The flavour of parenting influences the depth of the relationship between the child and parents.

These observations made me naturally inclined to reflect on my parents and their parenting. Did they preach? Did they control? Did they inspire? How did they shape me?

I realized that my parents were very subtle in their approach. They carried their lives the way they believed it to be. For an observant child like me, their lives were great sources of learning. As I look back, certain specific aspects cross my mind.

Their hard work to make a living – that too in an ethical manner – was exemplary. What we call a work ethic today is something that I picked up from my Dad. He stood by the principles, rules and guidelines of the organization. He was not afraid of speaking up to any authority. He was not ready to bend any rules to please people. He earned the tag of 'strict man'. He was also very committed to timelines and finishing work without any pendency.

When my Mom took up a job to augment family income, my Dad insisted she evolve into a worker with a similar work ethic—working hard, sticking to commitments, and never violating rules.

One more aspect of their parenting that touched me early in my life was my parents' financial discipline and philosophy of living within their means. They never pretended to be cash rich. At the same time, they never appeared to be sad, nor did they ever blame anyone for what their lives turned into.

They fulfilled the minimum requirements for festivals, celebrations, and family rituals. But they refrained from luxuries. The best part of their parenting was never making children feel deprived. I remember going shopping to buy clothes and sweets. My parents bought crackers for the Diwali festival at cheaper rates from their office co-operative. We had our education in decent schools (of course, no big brands). A big lesson from my parents was how to stay positive even when the financial situation was not looking bright.

Their frugal approach became a way of life, and I started exercising caution in how I spend money. This is a profound yet subtle influence of their parenting!

Another noteworthy teaching from my parents was how they played hosts to guests or relations. During my childhood, it was common to see my close uncles, aunts, or even distant cousins dropping into our house without notice for overnight stays. My Mom used to cook meals after a long day in the office. Parents made us arrange beds for the guests. It inculcated sensitivity towards guests in us. Anticipating the basic needs of the guests, placing them proactively, and making them feel at home have become our habits.

Reflecting today, I am fascinated with how my parents gradually created a sense of pride in my academic performance while initially being tolerant of my mediocre academic performance. They struck a very delicate balance. They ignited a desire to do well in academics, making me study studiously. However, when I performed below par, they did not punish me, shout at me, or make me feel worthless. They accepted me for what I was and motivated me to do better next time. It had a more profound impact and created a sense of ownership within me.

My heart fills with gratitude when I fondly recall the umpteen ways my parents shaped me. I learnt from them that parenting is not controlling, demanding, or expecting. It is all about nurturing, demonstrating values through their lives, and making children practice these values by creating hands-on experiences of life. My parents cared for me, not pampered; they wished for my success but never rejected me when I failed; they made me learn without preaching!

48

Cousins & Summers

These days, we hear a lot about rapport building, conversational skills, adaptability to different situations, relationship management, and so on.

In my case, just as in some of your lives, the foundation for most of these skills was laid during my summer holidays. After a year-long routine of going to school, doing homework, fearing the teachers and stressful examinations, I had every reason to wait for the vacation. Getting out of the house and travelling some seventy kilometres, or sometimes as short as twenty-five kilometres, was what I was looking forward to.

What was in that vacation that made me so excited? One obvious thing that I cherished was change. Often, we might think that change is uncomfortable, but seldom do we realize that routine is so boring and de-energizing. As I reflect now, I welcomed the summer vacations because of the new experiences that they offered.

Summer vacations were great opportunities for me to go beyond the confines of my home, school, and known circle of classmates. Rustic environments in rural areas, train journeys, and watching different people, their routines, and their constraints helped me to be more observant and a bit more sensitive.

I carry beautiful memories of experiences that helped me recharge myself during my childhood summers. Early morning walk to a water stream with cousins and the joyful jump to splash the water (though I did not and do not know how to swim), walking bare foot on mud roads, touching the glowing black skin of the buffaloes, eating previous night's rice with pickle and curd, gentle competition to grab more time to peddle the bicycle, playing games on the roads or open spaces, sleeping on the hard surface of the terrace in the night, watching the abundance of the sky and stars, listening to horror stories narrated by cousins, getting scared, praying to God and falling asleep....every experience was different from routine. I never experienced boredom.

When I look back, I cherish all those experiences and their significance in shaping me as a person. Those summer vacations taught me so many skills.

As simple as travelling alone without my parents prepared me to be independent. My added responsibility was to care for my sister, who is younger than me. Managing the small pocket money my parents gave us made me conscious of our spending. Keeping the count of my clothes and keeping them in an organized manner at my cousin's place was another learning. How many pairs of clothes were there, how many times I had to wash them for how many days of stay...these were simple calculations. I know these are all small trivia, but those were my early lessons in self-responsibility.

I was amazed at my adaptability during the summer vacations. When I was among many cousins, there was no pampering or special treatment. I had to adjust to some of the practices in my cousin's home. Let it be taking a bath near the well, eating food after serving the elderly, settling for one side dish only....I had to accept what was offered to all of us. I had no cosy bed, but I enjoyed sleeping on the terrace. Power cuts did not bother us because the moon and stars in the sky were giving us warm light. Even lanterns added beauty to our ambience. My cousins had different tastes, and they favoured different film personalities. While I backed my hero, I was also ready to listen to my cousins. I realized how much more we can learn by releasing our rigidity.

One more significant learning from my summers was observing how I developed greater comfort with some cousins than others; conversations with some cousins were much more flowing. Reasons could be mutual interest, empathy, and, essentially, compatibility of personalities.

As I write this piece, I realize how rich the contribution of my summers and cousins was in my life. Thanks to my parents, who encouraged me and my sister to go on such vacations, and thanks to my aunts, who welcomed a gang of cousins to assemble at their places during the summers. My aunts showed tremendous patience and showered so much love. Loving all children as their own was a great virtue.

That was real-time summer schooling for me!

49

Even Amitabh Had Flops!

To lead a lighter life, many people suggest that one should not take oneself too seriously. It is a simple yet profound statement for me. While I need a lot more time to contemplate this statement, I realized that I take myself quite seriously on the work front.

Whatever I take up, I must do a good job of it. When someone trusts me and assigns me some responsibility, I must fulfil the same with utmost sincerity. I should not allow others to point a finger at my lack of effort.

Those were my guiding principles and the defining features of my work ethic. While they may sound quite positive, they also place enormous pressure on me. Living up to someone's trust is a humungous responsibility.

Since I started working, my first reaction has always been self-doubt before I plunged into any assignment. Can I perform and satisfy the stakeholders? While I recognized the self-doubt, I seldom had a choice to avoid it. So, the only option left was to tackle my self-doubt, put in my sincere efforts and give my best. Whether it be making a conceptual presentation to a senior group, teaching a session for bright students of my age, launching a new initiative abroad, anchoring an additional responsibility of managing senior colleagues, etc.

I look back with wonderment at the amount of emotion that went into every assignment that I performed, especially when it was a new task that I never handled. I was not sure if it was my fear of failure, my deep desire for achievement, or my need for appreciation from others that drove me into those assignments emotionally. I may be unable to pinpoint which factor was the driving force, but I developed a strong emotion towards my work. I never learnt how not to take myself seriously.

Given the emotional investment, the joy was equally palpable upon completing every such assignment. Perhaps that was what I worked for.

Joy...yes, it was joyful whenever my efforts resulted in success and appreciation. What if it was a failure or the result was less than satisfactory? In my emotional investment to do my best in everything I take up, I do not think I prepared myself to deal with failures. I realized the same early in my career.

It was a teaching session that I worked hard to deliver. I did my best to prepare in terms of conceptual accuracy and depth. When I delivered the session, I did not experience a wow, a feeling of fulfilment (teachers always possess an internal compass to measure their happiness in teaching). Not that my students had any issues with my session, but I could sense a lack of energy. I felt I should have adopted a better teaching methodology to make my session more engaging instead of a serious-sounding and conceptually heavy session.

Naturally, I was disappointed with myself, though students did not complain in any way. It was my own feelings that were draining me and making me feel low. My inner chatter was, "I should have done better."

Towards the evening, I was walking out of the Institute campus and I bumped into my senior colleague, Ashish, a professor of Finance.

He was a warm person who always inquired about others. In no time, he sensed that I was low and that something was bothering me. He asked me in Hindi, "Kya hua?".

Given his warmth, I could not hide my feelings and opened up to him. "I am not happy with the way I handled today's session. I think it was a flop session," I said.

How he reacted to my statement and what he said got etched in my memory forever.

He affectionately patted me on the back and said, "Come on...you should not get disappointed or lose yourself with such one-off experiences. Even Amitabh Bachchan has had many flops in his career. Does it make him any less of a star? After one flop, he moves on and works harder for his next movie".

After saying this, Prof Ashish went home, leaving me with abundant positivity.

Striving for success is great, but learning to deal with failures and bouncing back is equally important.

50

Journey That Never Ends!

Writing this diary has been a fascinating journey of reflection. In this process, I realized that the smallest experiences have the immense potential to offer me great insights. My mindful pause and reflection are crucial in letting my life teach me and help me understand myself a bit more.

Having written a few episodes of reflections, can I say that I know myself fully? No way. I can find some patterns in some respects, but I have many more dilemmas in other aspects to resolve and many more layers of me to uncover.

Some of the many questions I want to explore cross my mind at this juncture.

Do I have regrets in life? I would be dishonest to say that I don't have regrets. When I think of some of my earlier actions or decisions, I do wish I had acted differently. But I do not worry about them. I do not experience emotions of disappointment or anger about the past, but I certainly learn and wish to do differently in future. So, I do not regret the past but learn from it.

Do I care for others? When I ponder my actions over the years, I realize I have done many things that might have helped people. Be it my teaching, coaching, supporting or advising...it would have impacted some people. Some of them did share and thanked me. However, I did all of that as a part of my work and commitment to my profession. Or I did those as a part of my roles in life. Does it mean I cared for others? Who did I care for? What did I do that was anything special towards others? I cannot recall any noteworthy gestures of caring for others. I feel I performed my duty.

Have I thanked enough? I don't think so. The more I take a 360-degree view of my life, the more humbled I become. As my age and experience grew, I recall how many people extended their helping hand – directly or indirectly; how many inspired and enabled me to become whatever I have become. A quick replay of all the episodes of life fills my heart with gratitude. Have I thanked all of them? Have I thanked enough? My inner voice responds with a firm no. I do not feel that I have expressed my gratitude enough. While I am always grateful, I have not verbalized. I wish my feelings of gratitude reach all those who shaped me!

Have I utilized my talents fully? The answer is a straight no. I believe I have more talent than what I utilized. Had

I pushed myself, I would have done much more. Then, what had stopped me? As I think of it now, perhaps my order of priority and some choices in life made me contended. I did not have the urge or that aggressive drive to achieve more. It must have been something to do with my definition of success as well.

Have I learnt enough? This is a very relative aspect. Compared to where I started, I have come a long way. Compared to what I could have learnt, my learning certainly falls short. My learning is directly proportional to my desire to keep myself fresh and engaged mentally!

Am I leaving any legacy behind? In the hierarchy of achievements, after my values, freedom and financial security, I certainly nurture the thought of leaving a legacy. When an organization that I worked for acknowledged my work and continued with my contribution even after my exit, it made me feel happy that I left a legacy. I felt remembered when a student accidentally met me and greeted me on the flight or in the mall. Yes, I nourished the thought of leaving a legacy, and I preserved those anecdotes wherever I felt I made a difference and left a legacy.

But as I kept observing the lives of various achievers, I wondered how many of them would be remembered for how long after they were gone from this world. We are all passing clouds to each other and experience fleeting emotions towards each other based on our needs and context. All this makes me reflect and leaves me with a philosophical thought of whether leaving a legacy is a strong enough purpose to live. Instead, make a difference to someone in some way while I am actively working – make a difference in the present instead of wishing to see the past remaining in the future. If at all there is some legacy, it must be our work and not our names.

I know. The last few paragraphs are all work in progress or philosophically evolving. I do not have firm perspectives. I continue to be engaged in this dialogue with myself.

My ordinary journey continues in search of extraordinary insights, and it will not end until I breathe last.

Thanks for reading through the pages of my diary.

I wish you too will reminisce those moments in your life that have immense potential to help us grow as a person.

Should you wish, you may write to me at drrajwrites@gmail.com to share your reflections and insights. I will be happy to personally read each of your mails and of course respect your privacy!